Essays on Early Newenden

Essays on Early Newenden

Åke Nilson

Published 2013 by
Friends of Saint Peter's Church, Newenden
A charity registered in England and Wales no. 1098260

Published by
Friends of Saint Peter's Church, Newenden
A charity registered in England and Wales no. 1098260
friends@newenden.org

ISBN 978-1492395805

Contents

Introduction

In February 2003, the Friends of Saint Peter's Church, Newenden, a secular charity for the maintenance and preservation of the fabric of the parish church, was established at a public meeting of the village. I had the honour of serving as the first Chairman of the Friends, as the charity is usually known, and its first ever fund-raising activity was a talk on local history by this Chairman.

These talks became an annual event, and have now been going for ten years. I have finally had the time and perhaps more importantly, enough grasp of the subject to be able to write them up into a more or less coherent document. That of course is not to say that it is a proper academic treatise – I am after all just an amateur in the field. No doubt, another ten years of research and thinking about how various aspects of the village are related will change my mind as much as the past ten years have.

The history of Newenden has always seemed fascinating – how come this tiny little village, with just over 200 inhabitants, had its own separate jurisdiction from the Middle Ages until not even 150 years ago? Was there really a Golden Age when Newenden had sixteen inns? What is Castle Toll and why does the church look so peculiar?

Introduction

The village certainly retains a feeling of being something special. It lies at the very interface between the Weald and the Marshes, and gets its character from both. It is one of the smallest parishes in Kent (1,046 acres or about 4 sq. km.) and is bounded to the south by the River Rother, which is also the county boundary with Sussex, and on the north by one of the Rother's major tributaries called Hexden Channel. Most of the houses nestle on the south side of the ridge between the waters and so see more of Sussex than they do of Kent. In more ways than one, therefore, it is a frontier settlement and this, in my view, is the key to its ancient riddles.

The great thing about English local history is that the material is almost limitless. There are volumes of records starting from the 13th century, which have hardly been touched, as well as very old records like the Anglo-Saxon Chronicle and Domesday Book, which give intriguing clues for further investigation. It does not take much research into the archives to find new facts that have never been placed into context before, especially if one can be privileged to constrain the enquiries to one small village.

Perhaps unfortunately, it also does not take much research to discover that a great deal of what has been written before is wrong, or at least misunderstood. To some extent, therefore, this document contradicts earlier writers on, I hope, reasonably solid grounds. Naturally, it wouldn't be a proper history if the author himself wasn't also able to introduce his own hypotheses. But at least I trust that, where the writing is pure speculation, this will be evident to the reader.

This is history, not biography, so it has been collected by subject into a series of essays, rather than strictly chronologically. It is also fairly heavily biased towards the earliest records of Newenden. This is partly by choice, because the earlier times seem more intriguing, partly because if there ever was a time when the village had a greater role to play, it

must have been in the 12th and 13th centuries, after which it declined to such an extent that Hasted could write of the
village, in 1798, that

> [t]he village, which is but small, consisting of a very few
> cottages ... [and] the greatest part of [the parish] is a low
> flat of pasture and marsh lands, the whole of it has a most
> forlorn and dreary aspect, and is far from being healthy.

In the first essay, *Origins*, I try to establish the age of the
settlement and how it came to be here. Then follow some
thoughts about the *Market*, which I believe was the cause of
Newenden's relative importance before the Black Death,
together with its location and communications, with which I
deal in *River, road and bridge*. If the place did have a time of
glory, it was during the reign of king Edward I, so the next
essay concerns *Edward I and his friends*. Of course, the King
and his noblemen may protest as much as they like, but the
village would not exist without a *Population*, which is the
following subject.

At this point, the reader will have faced an onslaught of
terms of mediaeval governance, so it may be appropriate to
explain them and how they apply to Newenden, which I
attempt in *Manors, Township and Liberty*. Finally, I deal with
the two oldest surviving monuments of village achievement,
which are the *Church* and, even older than that, *Castle Toll*.

There is a listing of Rectors of Newenden church as an
Appendix, as well as some maps to place the village in its
geographical neighbourhood.

No doubt, many readers will miss their favourite aspects of
village history. To them, I can only apologise – this was never
intended to be a complete history of Newenden, just a summary of what I have found over the last ten years' occasional
forays into the archives. Especially for the more recent

Introduction

history, I recommend the books listed in the bibliography, which are sources both of information and inspiration.

I must thank those kind people who have helped and inspired me more directly. They include (without any aspirations to completeness) Tim Asay at the University of Oregon, Hans Helander and Monica Hedlund, professors of Latin at Uppsala University; Mike Berry, Muguette Bourne, Helen and Tony Cloote, Peter Cyster, Rosie and Hugh Edmonds, Kathy and Chris Turnbull in the village; Chris Willis of the Friends; Judy Vinson of the Parish Magazine; Mark Bateson at Canterbury Cathedral Archive who started me off on the research, and many other staff and volunteers at archives and libraries I have visited.

And of course Ingrid, without whose patience, tolerance and encouragement nothing would ever get done.

Origins

All works on Newenden history start by claiming that the first record of the village is in a charter made by King Offa in 791, granting the manor of Newenden to the prior and monks of Christ Church, Canterbury.

Unfortunately, they are all wrong.

A misread with long-term consequences

The charter referred to has the index number S 1614[1], and now exists in five manuscript copies. It is in Latin[2] and relatively short. Translated[3], it says something like:

> In the year of our Lord 791. I, King Offa, give to Christ Church Canterbury property consisting of 15 plough-lands in the province of Kent in the places named hereafter, that is Ickham, Palmstead and Ruckinge, and in the forest called Andred pasture for swine in these places: Dunwalingden, Sandhurst, Swithelmingden and in the woods called *Bocholt* and *Blean Heanhric* and another between the rivers Northburn and *Hagenatreou* and pasture for one flock next to Thanington, and fifty swine at Smeeth. This, the aforesaid gift I give to Christ Church with all that belongs thereto, free of any royal taxation. If

anybody attempts to infringe on this gift, may he be for-
ever excommunicated.

The sharp-eyed reader will note the striking absence of any
reference to Newenden[4]. To explain this, first bear in mind
that these manuscripts are written in a clerical minuscule
which can be very hard to decipher. In particular, letters like i,
n, m and u which consist just of short strokes of the pen
(called *minims*) are easily confused. The transliteration on
which the text above is based is the best that modern scholars
can produce, but in earlier times, the reading of this
manuscript has been different. In particular, Dunwalingden[5]
has been read in other ways.

At some point somebody, perhaps Lambarde[6], read this
name as *Di nivalnydene*, noted the proximity of Sandhurst
and came to the conclusion that it referred to Newenden. The
idea was that the origin of the name Newenden might be a
Saxon name *Nifeldune*, which would mean the low or deep
valley. There are some problems with this hypothesis, not
least that the river valley is hardly low or deep at Newenden
(and there is also the pesky *Di* word, which doesn't seem to
go anywhere).

Dunwalingden, on the other hand, is easy to explain:
Dunwal is a Saxon name, the Dunwalings are his family or
perhaps his men, and the -*den* part in Wealden place-names
means a glade in the forest which was used for swine pasture
in the summer. So Dunwalingden is just the *den* of Dunwal's
people. This place can't be found any longer – perhaps it has
really ceased to exist, or perhaps the name has morphed into
something else – maybe Dingleden, just north of Sandhurst?

However, the ancient, now discarded reading is the origin
of the idea that Newenden was first mentioned in 791. It has
been repeated by author after author, although oddly enough,
it would be quite easy (but still wrong) by the very same
token to say that the village was first mentioned in 785, as

there is another charter[7] by King Offa where he gives the same properties to his minister Ealdbeorht and the minister's sister Selethryth, who became the abbess of Lyminge[8].

One wonders why Offa withdrew the gift to give it away to Canterbury instead? Offa, who was King of Mercia, became the overlord of Kent in the 760's, but after his death in 796, the Kentish royal family re-established their position. The new Kentish king Cuthred in 805 granted two plough-lands in Ruckinge to the same Ealdbeorht and Selethryth, quite possibly in part compensation[9].

Lossenham

The first mention of any place in Newenden parish is in another charter, number S 1180, which dates from 11 July 724. Here Æthelberht, son of the Kentish King Wihtred, gave to Abbess Mildred a grant of one plough-land around the river Limen[10], as well as a meadow at *Hammespot*. At the end of this charter, after the signatures, is a list of the swine pastures apparently covered by the donation, and this includes *Hlossanham*. It would appear that this list was added later, either by way of clarification, or perhaps even by the recipient trying to add to the gift after the fact. Even so, it seems reasonably likely that Lossenham did exist at the time.

-Ham in Anglo-Saxon place-names means home or homestead and places ending in *-ham* are among the oldest Anglo-Saxon settlements. There is some dispute over the meaning of the first part of the name, though. The often quoted authority on English place-names, Ekwall[11] suggests a personal name *Hlossa*, so that Lossenham would be "Hlossa's *ham*". However, according to Wallenberg[12] (another Swedish expert on place-names – it seems this was a popular subject at Uppsala University in the 1930s), the problem is that no reference has ever been found to that name before or since.

He instead suggests that the name may come from OE *hlosa*, a listener, watchman or spy (the word is related to OE *hlosnian* or "listen" in modern English). With the place situated at the Kentish border to Sussex, which was populated by people of a different and not unconditionally friendly origin, this seems quite possible. The civilisation of the Jutes in Kent is considered to have been fairly well developed, and may have been in some way related to the culture of the Rhineland, whereas the South Saxons seem to have been rather a rough lot[13]. The mysterious Castle Toll (see the final essay, p.73) at the very end of the ridge could perhaps have started out as such a listening post.

First written reference to Newenden

The place-name simply means "the new *den*", or forest pasture. The first mention is in a review of the Archbishop's manors in Kent[14], dating from between 1070 and 1082 (and thought most likely to be from the earlier part of this period). This document, which is a contemporary record of proceedings in the shire court, includes the following sentence:

> *Langport et neuuenden de archiepiscopatu est, et archiepiscopus dedit goduino, et episcopus statim in placito cognouit esse de ecclesia.*

Which means, roughly:

> Langport [the hundred in which Lydd is situated] and Newenden belong to the Archbishop, and the Archbishop gave them to [Earl] Godwin, and the bishop now pleads that they should be deemed held by the Church.

By that time, the village was well established, and the manor of Newenden had already been granted by the King to the Archbishop, so it must have been founded some time earlier.

The Archbishop then found the manor valuable enough to be worth giving to Godwin, the powerful Earl of Wessex. He died in 1053 and had not been in favour for a couple of years before that, so we can safely say that the latest possible date for Newenden's foundation is the early 11th century, but it is probably a century or two older than that.

In one of William the Conqueror's obituaries[15] from 1087, Langport and Newenden are again mentioned (among many other places in Kent and elsewhere) as having been restored to Canterbury by him – something particularly laudable in the view of the obituary's unknown author – so the court case recorded above likely went well for the bishop.

A hypothesis about the origin of Newenden

Older historians had a tendency to think up amazing ideas for the origins of Newenden, but these are now generally discredited. The theory that Newenden was a Roman city called *Noviodunum* fails because no Roman coins or other artefacts have been found here. (There is only one reference to Roman coins being found around Newenden, and this is by Mr R.C. Hussey, who said at a meeting of the Archaeological Institute in 1858, that "[Roman] coins are occasionally brought to light in the neighbourhood of Newenden"[16], but I can find no other evidence of these coins.) And the view that Newenden was *Anderida*, a Romano-British stronghold, is also out of favour, with *Anderida* now usually located at Pevensey.

So we must take Newenden at its Anglo-Saxon face value.

There are many Kentish place-names ending in -*den*, especially in the Weald. The places to which they refer generally belonged to people living outside the great forest, and were used in summer only, for swine to fatten up on oak and beech mast. The swine were driven along ancient tracks from their winter quarters, sometimes far away (after all, Tenterden is the modern name for *Tanetwaraden*, the *den* of the men of Thanet), to spend the growing season feeding in the lush forest, being watched over by a swineherd, often a young person left to fend for himself for several months. Moving livestock from winter to summer quarters is an agricultural practice known as transhumance, and it was common in many parts of Europe.

However, Newenden seems an odd place to keep a lightly guarded flock of swine in the summer. It is at the very edge of the forest, and it is also just on the border with Sussex, so any rustlers would find it easy to escape with their captures. Also, other *dens* tend to be located on high ground (e.g. Rolvenden and Tenterden), perhaps so that the poor swineherd could get some warning of an impending attack and at least have a chance to run away himself. A further observation is that many of the neighbouring *dens* do not have their own entries in Domesday Book[17] (nor does Lossenham), even though they certainly existed at the time. The reason for this is that they were counted as a property of the parent manor, and so the income of the *den* was described as part of the parent's agricultural activities. But Newenden was independent enough to have its own entry. Also, Newenden is very near Lossenham – the distance between St. Peter's Church in Newenden and Lossenham Manor is not even half a mile, as the pig wanders, which is much less than the usual distance between bigger settlements.

Finally, if you consider a map of Newenden parish (p.85), you will see that Lossenham is situated more or less exactly in the middle. Although manors did not necessarily have a geo-graphical definition, it is striking that the piece of land which later became defined as the Township (more of this later, p.60), and which must have corresponded to the area where the writ of Newenden manor ran, as opposed to that of

Lossenham manor, is confined to a small corner next to the river. It very much looks like a chunk of the original land that has been set aside for a special purpose.

All of this makes me think that perhaps Newenden is not a *den* in the usual sense. It is my conjecture that Newenden is an offshoot of Lossenham. Perhaps the people of Lossenham realised that the lowest point where it is possible to cross the river by means of a causeway and bridge would make for an excellent border crossing and market place. They created a new settlement and called it "the new place" – Newenden – because by this time, perhaps in the late 9th or 10th century, the *dens* were no longer just agricultural summer stations, but had become villages in their own right. The meaning of the word had been diluted and could indicate any sort of location (as indeed it does today – many houses are given -*den* names without the least connection with swine). Once "the new place" had become established, it turned out to be a much more interesting place to be, so the population, and with it the focus of the parish moved to the land around the river crossing.

Market

There is a great deal of evidence for the mediaeval market in Newenden. A weekly market was not something found in every settlement, but was reserved for the *burhs*. This Anglo-Saxon word is usually translated as "borough" and means a town, with walls and a generally urban character. There were eight of them in Kent by the time of Domesday Book: Canterbury, Rochester, Sandwich, Hythe, Fordwich, Seasalter, Dover and Romney. But in addition, Domesday Book tells of four other places with markets: Newenden, Faversham, Dartford and Lewisham. So there were only twelve markets in the whole county, possibly fifteen as there is also other documentary evidence of markets at Eastbridge, Lenham and Malling[18].

Indeed, when the Norman kings got hold of the administration, they formally restricted the setting up of new markets, to prevent newcomers from inflicting commercial damage on the existing markets. The rule was that no market could be set up within a day's walk of another, and this seems to have been the case even before the Conquest. There were a number of other strict rules on how market trades should be carried out, generally setting certain price levels or maximum profits allowed, as well as prohibiting manipulation of market prices by causing artificial shortages, or re-selling goods already bought at the same market[19]. There was also the Assize of Bread and Ale, which was a statute introduced by Henry III regulating the price of ale and the weight of a farthing loaf of bread. The enforcement of this statute could be delegated to the lord of the manor where the market was held, and this appears to have been the case for Newenden. It was quite possibly part of the reason why the village was given township status (of which more later, p.60).

In Domesday Book, Newenden market is recorded as worth (in rent to the manor holder) 40 shillings less 5 pence, that is £1.19s.7d.[20] By comparison, the market in Faversham was worth £4, twice as much. Faversham is in a much more populated part of the county[21], especially in those days, when the Weald was still difficult pioneer country, at least compared to the long-settled lands on the Downs and the North Kent coast.

By 1312, Godfrey le Waleys was the direct lord of Newenden manor, and he held a market on Thursdays, which he claimed his ancestors had held "from time out of mind"[22]. The Waleys family had indeed been the holders of the manor for quite some time and more of their connection with Newenden will be found in the essay on Edward I and friends (p.42ff).

In a letter from 1313[23] Archbishop Winchelsey complains, not for the first time, over the markets in Newenden and Tenterden "which for two days cause disgrace because of the egregious behaviour of the people" so close to the respective churches. Robert Winchelsey was a forceful man, who became Archbishop of Canterbury in 1293. He was probably from Winchelsea, as his name indicates, but this is not known for sure. He fell out with Edward I in the long-running struggle between the Crown and the Church over taxation and tithes, to the point of being forced into exile in 1305. When the king died in 1307, Winchelsey returned to England, but soon fell out with the new king as well, this time over

Edward II's favourite Piers Gaveston, of whom Winchelsey strongly disapproved. He died in May 1313, not long after the letter about the uncouth markets – a communication fully in keeping with the forthright views of this powerful and out-spoken Archbishop.

Presumably the market was situated along the road just below the church, where it would be most easily accessible for traders and customers. No doubt, the people coming to the market to buy and sell, after finishing their tasks felt a need to celebrate their bargains, or maybe just to clear their throats after much shouting and haggling. This is the time when it is said that there were sixteen inns in the village (sometimes, you even see the figure fifty-two). In mediaeval times, many people brewed their own ale and, when it was ready to drink, they placed a green bush or branch outside the house, to advertise that anybody could come in and buy a pint. If this sort of establishment counts as an inn, then it is perhaps not surprising that their numbers could and indeed would need to be quite large.

At this point, there was evidently a market in Tenterden as well. The earlier restrictions on new markets had been lifted and competition for Newenden market was growing rapidly. It came principally from Tenterden and Cranbrook, which were building up their wealth on the wool trade. In 1331, Edward III invited Flemish weavers to Kent, and Tenterden, in particular, profited from their skills to start producing woollen broadcloth[24]. Appledore, too, gained a market. After the Black Death in the middle of the 14th century, the re-sulting scarcity of workers meant that agriculture moved away from arable towards sheep farming, which was both less labour-intensive and more in demand, as a result of the cloth business, and therefore a great deal more profitable. Newenden's mostly marshy fields were not suited to sheep, and so the village and its market declined.

Further commercial competition came in 1383, when Sir Edward Dallingridge[25] was granted, by royal charter dated 25 February[26], the right to hold a market at Bodiam. Dallingridge had become wealthy from plundering the French countryside during the Hundred Years' War, and when he came back to England, he applied for royal permission to crenellate (that is, to fortify) his manor house at Bodiam. This permission was granted on 21 October 1385, and also included the right to build a castle nearby[27]. This, of course, became the spectacular Bodiam Castle – by many considered the very epitome of a mediaeval castle.

The last reference to Newenden in this context comes from the Patent Rolls for Richard II, which show on 3 February 1385 a grant for life to William Kyng of various property, including the fair of Newenden "as held by John Walsshe by gift of the duke of Brittany, for whose rebellion the said ... fair [is] in the king's hands." This John Walsshe would have been called John le Waleys at the beginning of the century, and was possibly the grandson of Godfrey (see also the story of the Waleys family).

Note that this grant refers to a *fair* of Newenden, not a market. Markets were weekly, but fairs were normally held only once annually, typically on the day of the saint to which the village church was dedicated. It is of course possible that the scribe was mistaken about the character of the event in Newenden, but it seems more likely that the weekly market was no longer held and that an annual fair was a mere echo of what once had been.

Nonetheless, the Newenden fair was valuable enough to have been given to the Duke of Brittany, when he was in favour. (He also must have sub-let it straight back to the Waleyses.) This duke would have been John Montfort (the fifth duke of this name), who had an interesting life, to put it mildly. He first had to fight off the House of Blois in the

Breton War of Succession (1341-1364) to gain the dukedom, which he only managed with help from the English. He married Mary Plantagenet, who was a daughter of Edward III, but she died shortly after the marriage. In the circumstances, it was not surprising that he granted many Breton manors to English barons, which was also helpful for them in the Hundred Years' War against France. However, the Breton nobles resented this and with their agreement, the French king Charles V put such pressure on Brittany that John had to flee into exile with his former father-in-law in England in 1373. Then Charles tried to annex the duchy completely into France, at which point the Breton nobles rather regretted having invited him, and instead asked John to come back. He returned in 1379 and regained control with the help of a threatening English army approaching from Calais. But then Charles died and his young son came to the throne as Charles VI in 1380. John paid off the English army and reconciled with the young Charles, which may be the "rebellion" referred to by Richard II (who was himself only 16 years old, and perhaps prone to seeing rebellion everywhere, having just seen off the Peasants' Revolt in 1381).

Newenden market, though once a minor chip in the game of international politics, faded away and was not heard of again.

River, road and bridge

The first road through Newenden long pre-dates the village itself. It is the ridge-way from Ticehurst and beyond, via Flimwell, Hawkhurst and Sandhurst. It is probably pre-Roman, from when people first started making use of the resources of the vast forest. The road is still there, now known as the A268, and faithfully follows the top of the ridge all the way to Newenden. It seems likely that the road originally continued along what is today Frogs Hill Lane all the way out towards the end of the ridge, where Castle Toll stands.

Lossenham was then settled along the road and when (as I believe) Newenden was later created as a market place by the river, the road was forked to serve the new settlement and provide a connection for trade with Sussex. By the time of the Norman invasion, the road network in and around the modern parish was pretty much in place already, providing links with Tenterden and the Kentish heartland to the north, with Rye and Winchelsea to the south, and to Sandhurst, Hawkhurst and ultimately London to the west.

Together with the market, the road with the bridge and the river traffic were the main reasons for Newenden's significance in mediaeval times. Winchelsea was, in its great days between about 1200 and 1400, the most important port on the English south coast and the road from London to Winchelsea and Rye, which took over Winchelsea's role as premier Channel port in the 16th century, passed through Newenden. Here is the lowest point at which the Rother could be crossed without using a ferry (at least during those periods when the bridge was in good repair). Though the roads through the Weald were notoriously bad, some types of traffic had to use them, as the sea route would take too long. The rippiers (fishmongers) of Rye, carrying their catch to London for sale there, used the road via Newenden and were able to get fresh fish to the capital in a day of hard riding. In 1710, it was reported that some 300 rippiers' horses passed Tunbridge Wells every day en route from Rye and Hastings northwards[28].

A rippier of Rye called James Wilford, who later became a Merchant Taylor and alderman of London, was so fed up with this particular road that, in his will of 1514[29], he gave a perpetual annuity of £9.13s.4d. in the form of rents charged on the Saracen's Head property (nos. 5, 6 and 7 Friday Street[30] – between Cannon Street and Queen Victoria Street in the City of London) which was owned by the Merchant Taylors' company. This enabled a yearly payment of £7 to be used for the repair of the road between Riverhill and Northiam Church "upon the information of the parishioners of Northiam, Newenden and Rye". Incidentally, it is not altogether clear which Riverhill is being referred to. The only possible location so called now is the hill up on the southern side of the Greensand Ridge at Sevenoaks, but that is a long way away and the repair money seems generally to have been used in the Newenden–Northiam area – even in the 16th century £7 wouldn't have made much difference if employed equally all the way from Sevenoaks.

In 1924, the annuity was redeemed for £280 worth of Consols[31], but the trust continued, still paying £7 p.a. as per the original will. Payments were made to Newenden resident Herbert Relf in 1927, 1930, 1931 and 1933 for repairing fences.

In 1936, the trust was converted into two charities, one for Kent and one for East Sussex[32]. Amazingly, they are still operating, 500 years after the original donation, and are now managed by the respective counties' Highways Authorities.

The Rother

It is worth noting that the river is very old and it is the eroding power of the Rother, or *Limen* as it was anciently called, together with its tributaries, that has worn down the Wealden rocks to give the landscape the shape it has today. During the Ice Age, when vast volumes of water were frozen into the great ice-caps further north (the ice never reached Newenden's latitude), the sea level was as much as 120 metres lower than it is now. The river was flowing in the same course then as now, and in fact, the continuation of its prehistoric bed can be traced on the bottom of Rye Bay. In the present valley, the river gnawed its way into the bedrock far below its current level. This also explains why the relatively small river has such a wide valley. It has been created by the river and the tides over a very long period and it is filled with silt, both marine and fluvial, to a depth of 30 metres[33].

A great deal has been written about the course of the Rother across the marshes in ancient times and, tempting though the subject is, it is only of marginal relevance to the history of Newenden. Suffice to say that, at the time when the village was founded, the river flowed north of the Isle of Oxney, past Appledore and then in a great bend south not too far from the present-day location of Rye, then turning north-east to reach the sea at Romney. But then, during a series of storms in the 13th century, the river found a new outlet to the sea through a breach in the great shingle wall that once blocked off all of Rye Bay and the marshes, from Pett to Hythe. For instance, in 1256 there is a mention[34] that "the river of Niwenden is diverted by inundation of the sea", which must have been the result of an earlier storm. Unfortunately for Winchelsea, this breach was right where the old town was located, possibly more or less where the outermost pier-heads at the mouth of the river stand today, and the great storm of 1287 finally obliterated Old Winchelsea.

The breach in the shingle wall widened rapidly, giving the sea direct access up the low-lying levels around the Isle of Oxney and far into the Rother and Hexden valleys on either side of the Newenden ridge. The river became tidal all the way to Bodiam (as it still would be today, if it were not for the lock at Scots Float, near Rye) and the sea inundated great tracts of agricultural land. By 1332, 650 acres were permanently under salt water – an area approximately two-thirds the size of Newenden parish.

At this point, the landowners on either side of the river, Isabella Aucher at Lossenham and Geoffrey de Knelle – whose name tells you where he lived, just over on the Sussex side – decided to take drastic action. They built a great wall, which became known as the Knelle Dam, across the river valley from the Sussex side to the Isle of Oxney, in order to force the river to flow north of the Isle, and also to stop the salt-water from drowning the levels. Permission was given by the King by letter dated 7 March 1332[35]. Today, the dam is known as Bush Wall and can still be seen in the landscape. It is visible just east of New Barn, an ancient and isolated farmstead at the eastern end of the parish, then carries on via Maytham Wharf to Potman's Heath, where the Rolvenden to Wittersham road actually runs on top of the dam (past the cottage next to the bridge over what is today the Newmill Channel).

This dam had the wanted effects, but also an unexpected and unwanted effect, which was that it slowed down the river so much that the levels now became inundated with freshwater instead, and also hindered navigation from the upper reaches of the river down to the sea. Despite complaints, a Commission of Sewers in 1347 decided that the dam on balance was an asset rather than a liability, and so it remained in place. Newenden landowners had to live with much of their property being permanently under water. Eventually 3,000 acres in "Newenden levels", which would be the levels between Bodiam and Reading – this is equal to three times the surface of Newenden parish today – were described as "drowned lands".

On the other hand, the port of Newenden now became more important. Certainly, there had always been wharves and shipping activity here, but with the market fading away, and traditional agriculture losing its importance both because of the inundation of much of the land, and also because of the previously described move to sheep-farming, the barge traffic to Rye and other ports along the river became a major occupation of the village. There was ship-building at Reading and Smallhythe, which required both large timber from the mighty oaks of the great forest, and cannon, made in the Wealden foundries. With Newenden situated where one of the few comparatively usable roads out of the Weald reaches the river, it seems reasonable to think that both timber and iron products were transhipped onto barges here and then carried down to the shipyards and further.

However, Newenden probably never was a major port – if it had been, it would likely have been invited to join the Cinque Ports, as Smallhythe was (the reason why Tenterden lays claim to being a member of that illustrious confederation). Of course, being a "limb" of the Cinque Ports also carried with it obligations to supply and man ships, and the village being too small and poor to fulfil such demands may well have been another reason.

If there is one thing the Wealden rivers can be relied upon, it is their ability to scrape silt from the soft sandstone over which they run, and carry it downstream where it causes havoc with man's navigational efforts. This, together with the "inning" of land (the reclamation of land from the sea and freshwater courses) eventually caused the channel north of the Isle of Oxney to shrink to the point where, in the latter half of the 16th century, it became impossible to carry on ship-building at Smallhythe. Nonetheless, as late as 1549, Henry VIII had a 400-ton ship called *Grand Masters* built there[36]. Other effects were even further inundation of land in the Newenden levels, and the silting up and decline of Rye harbour.

In 1600, the build-up of water above Newenden caused the Knelle Dam to burst, and the river emptied down through the Wittersham levels to the south of the Isle. Although the land-owners from Newenden up were delighted to retrieve some of the "drowned lands", the Wittersham people suffered the reverse effect, so it was decided to rebuild the dam again. But the time had clearly come to do something about the state of the river. A new Commission of Sewers was appointed in 1609 with the task of draining the levels and making the river navigable again. Vast amounts of effort and money were ex-pended in channelling and other works until 1624, but to little effect, except for causing a local boom for dam-builders and general labourers in Newenden.

There was only one thing to do, and after much persuasion, the landowners in Wittersham agreed. In 1635, the Knelle Dam was deliberately breached and the river started flowing south of the Isle of Oxney again. Further work in the 1680's fixed the river to its current course in the Craven Channel down to Scots Float, and since then, the river has been much as we see it today (except that the extraction of water for agricultural and domestic purposes has reduced the flow considerably).

Barge traffic to Newenden Wharf continued until about 1933, with Rye sailing barges measuring 45ft in length, 12ft wide and drawing only 2ft 6ins – the limits were imposed by the size of the lock[37] at the old Scots Float sluice, built in 1844 and replaced by the current construction in 1986. The barges could carry about 20 tons. In the beginning of the 19th century, there were up to 16 barges employed on the Rother, sailing or being towed as far as Bodiam[38].

Newenden Bridge

The first reference I can find to a bridge and causeway at Newenden is from 1332[39], where the risk of undermining of the causeway is mentioned in the letter authorising the Knelle Dam, but it seems likely the bridge had been in existence before that. By 1365, however, we find a complaint[40] that

> whereas there should be, and of ancient times was, a bridge over the water flowing at the place of Newenden over which fishermen and others of those parts used to pass, which bridge men of both counties used to repair has long been broken, and for this cause some men having lands on both sides of the water have made a ferry boat and take certain customs from all passing by the boat to the simple profit of the lords of the boat, and so for default of repair of the bridge the men of both counties sustain no small loss and find who ought to make and repair such bridge.

This will have been a result of the freshwater inundation occasioned by the Knelle Dam, as described above. That there was a causeway (this is the raised roadbed along which the A28 still runs from the bridge to the K&ESR railway station in Northiam) already in the 14th century shows that the river must have been fairly well confined to its main course before the great storms of 1287 and earlier, otherwise the causeway would surely have been washed away by spring tides from time to time. In the early 14th century, there are several references to "the sea coast" between Newenden and other places – which shows that the river valley had by then become an inlet of the sea and therefore subject to much greater forces.

The bridge must have been re-built at some point, or perhaps on several occasions, but I have found no further significant references to it until 1637, when the river was again flowing normally after the opening of the Knelle Dam and the time evidently had come to undertake a major bridge renovation.

Camden writes[41], in that year, but presumably based on an earlier visit:

> I saw nothing there now, but a mean village with a poore Church, & a wodden bridge to no great purpose for a ferry is in most use, since that the river Rother, not containing himselfe in his chanell hath overlaied, & is like to endanger & surround the levell of rich lands thereby.

However, improvements were on their way. In April 1637, there was an order[42] at the Lewes Quarter Sessions that

> It is agreed between the said Counties that said Edward B[oyce?] shall [illegible] the said Bridge three score foot in length whereof the middle Arch to be twentysix foot and the other two Arches seventeen foot across and the same to be erected and set up at the Place where the old Bridge now stands without removing of the old Foundation...

This is particularly interesting because it shows that this 1637 bridge was built on the old, perhaps mediaeval foundation and also because the proportions of the new bridge sound very much like those of the present bridge.

There is a corresponding order from Maidstone in July the same year[43], which authorises a payment of thirty-six pounds, though for the "repairing" of the bridge. Perhaps this is a reflection of the fact that the new construction was based on the old foundation. Since Kent and Sussex were each liable for half the cost of any works to Newenden bridge, as it straddles the county border, this means the total cost came to £72. Though that doesn't sound a great deal, the total cost in 1701 of re-building the church east wall and building a new tower came to £57 and a bit, which shows that these bridge works must have been more than just routine repairs.

Then the present bridge was built in 1706, as the now rather badly eroded inscription says (it can be found in the middle of the bridge, on the inside of the downstream parapet). Maidstone archive has repair orders from 1704 and 1707, but the main payment seems to have been made by order of the Quarter Sessions in March 1710[44], where the sum of £109.19s.4d. was authorised, again for "repairing" the bridge but clearly for more substantial work – the total of nearly £220 is around three times as much as the 1637 payment, even taking into account inflation during the intervening period.

Despite all the money spent, the bridge became "dangerous to pass" in 1732 and new paving and pointing was required, as well as the spreading of 19½ tons of beach (i.e. shingle, or gravel, for readers not from this area). Then, in 1769, a survey found that

> the East and West Buttresses and the North Core thereof are greatly decayed insomuch that had the Repairs of the Bridge been deferred the Arches would in a short Time have given Way...

During WWII, the bridge was mined, so that it could easily be blown up in case of a German invasion, which might well have landed at the flat beaches of Romney and proceeded up the Rother valley towards London. In order to prevent the parapets from damping the explosion, these were removed and carefully stored, all individual stones numbered, to be replaced after the end of the war. Then, in 1982, with the arrival of 40+ tonne lorries, it was decided to replace the foundation of the bridge, and the old oak piles on which the bridge had rested at least since 1706, possibly since 1637 or even earlier, were removed and replaced with a concrete raft. But the three-hundred year old superstructure, based on a design seventy years older than that, is still there and serving its purpose well[45].

The Turnpike

Though the Wealden roads were infamous for their horrible state, especially in wintertime, the old ridge-way through Newenden may have been of relatively good quality, due to following the top of the hills rather than dipping down into the many river valleys.

Once the armed forces started making serious demands on the roads for the transport of cannon and other heavy items (such as oak timbers for ships), something needed to be done. In 1555, the Statute for Mending of Highways provided that every parish was to be responsible for the state of its own roads, and that all householders had to work on the roads for eight hours on four days every year; this was increased to six days in 1562. Each person holding land worth £50 p.a. also had to supply a team consisting of a cart with horses or oxen, plus two men. Each parish would elect, every Easter week, two people to be "surveyors and orderers" for the year. From 1662, the surveyors and orderers could also levy a highway rate not exceeding sixpence per pound rateable value. This system lasted until 1835, when it was abolished through the Highway Act, which introduced permanent parish surveyors, who could levy rates on landowners to pay for keeping the roads in good repair.

Especially for this part of the world, there were also the Wealden Road Acts of Henry VIII, which established a fee payable by the iron-masters for each load dispatched.

Despite this, the roads remained problematic. At the beginning of the 18th century, a new concept was introduced: the Turnpike Trust. It was decided that businessmen with an interest in good roads would be allowed to club together and create turnpikes, that is private toll roads open to the public for a small fee, in return for the obligation of keeping the roads up to a high standard. These trusts were established by Act of Parliament and by the middle of the century, so many of them were being started in the Weald that the period is sometimes referred to as the "Turnpike Mania" (1750-1770, more or less).

One of the trusts to be established in this period was for turnpiking the road from Flimwell to Rye, via Newenden and Northiam, by Act of Parliament 1762[46]. The reason for allowing the turnpike (the system was not always popular with poorer road users, and there were actual anti-turnpike riots in the West Country – but not in the Weald) was stated to be that the road because of "Deepness of the Soil" and "many heavy Carriages frequently passing and repassing ... loaded with Timber and Guns for Naval and Ordnance Service"

> is very ruinous and bad and in the Winter Season almost impassable, and other Parts thereof by Reason of their Narrowness are very incommodious and Dangerous to Travellers.

In addition to the main stretch from Flimwell to Rye, the Act also permitted the trust to include side roads from Highgate in Hawkhurst to Cooper's Corner in Salehurst and to Tubb's Lake in Cranbrook. These now form part of the A229. At the first renewal of the Trust, in 1783, the northern side road was withdrawn from the Trust's jurisdiction, but then in 1791, Whitbread Lane was added. This is the "short-cut" from just above the present K&ESR railway station in Northiam through to Beckley. Before then, the turnpike route was via the centre of Northiam and on to Beckley along what is now the B2088.

There were some 200 trustees named in the Act, including members of the Frewen family of Brickwall in Northiam, who were related by marriage to the Bishop family here, as well as Robert and James Monypenny of Rolvenden. The list was headed by Robert Fairfax, 7th Lord Fairfax of Cameron, who is mostly famous for owning 21,380 sq. km (some 5 million acres) of North American soil – which he inherited just as the American Revolution had confiscated the land. But somewhat more relevant to us, his mother was a Culpeper, a family which had held Lossenham manor until 1628. To be a trustee, you had to have an annual income of £40, or be heir to an estate worth £100 p.a., or yourself have estate worth £1,000. This might explain why there were no Newenden residents among the trustees – hardly any of them were that wealthy. The Act also established that the trustees were to meet at the Sign of the Six Bells in Northiam, which they faithfully did until the end of the Trust.

The Act authorised the Trust to establish three toll bars between Flimwell and Newenden Bridge, and three between there and Rye, as well as one on each side road. One of these bars, or turnpikes, was in Newenden and the toll cottage built for the toll collector stood on the corner of Lossenham Lane. It was pulled down in 1961 to make space for the petrol station – which is no longer there either.

Tolls applied only to coaches and carriages and to animals, not to pedestrians. They ranged from 1 shilling for coaches drawn by six horses, to threepence for a small landau drawn by a single horse. A single horse, not pulling a coach or waggon was charged at a penny, and droves of cattle at fivepence per score, whereas hogs and sheep cost twopence per score. These tolls were doubled in the period between 1 October and 1 May, and were payable at *each* toll bar. So a winter traveller in a six-horse coach would have paid twelve shillings for the pleasure of driving from Rye to Flimwell – not a small amount of money. However, return journeys on the same day were free.

There were of course exemptions; these mostly applied for one toll bar only. For example, free passage was allowed for agricultural transports by locals, for going to church, for soldiers and MPs (funny that, some things do not appear to change through the centuries) and, significantly, for unladen carriages of fish returning from London.

The income could only be used (1) for the cost of passing the Act and (2) for erecting turnpikes, toll houses and for repairing roads, but for no other purpose, except that the Trust would be allowed to have a Clerk, a Treasurer, Collectors and Surveyors and these could be paid an allowance. The officials had to account for all moneys received, or be taken to gaol in Kent or Sussex until they were prepared to produce the accounts.

Powers were granted for 21 years initially, and there were very many more provisions, including the obligation to measure the roads and place milestones each mile, showing the distance from London.

In the returns for 1820, the distance from Flimwell to Rye was declared at 17 miles, 3 quarters and 11 rods, which is unchanged today, going via Whitbread Lane. The original route was about 1 ½ mile longer. The average income over the previous three years had been £1,331.3s.7d. and the average expenditure £888.8s.10d. There were now 161 trustees and the Trust had an outstanding mortgage of £5,445[47].

The Trust was finally closed in 1872 and the final accounts[48] showed income £589 and expenditure £517. This included salaries of the Treasurer: £5; the Clerk: £15; and the Surveyor: £35. After the last £350 of the debt had been paid off, there remained a balance of £219, which was divided between the Clerk: £45; the Surveyor: £105 and the remainder went to the various Highway Authorities whose responsibility the road would henceforth be.

Edward I and his friends

There are at least two reasons for focusing somewhat on Edward I, king of England from 1272 to 1307. First, he is the only monarch with whom there is any Newenden connection. Second, it was probably during his reign that the village reached the apex of its importance as a settlement. It is of course quite possible that those two reasons are related.

Various record entries prove beyond doubt that Edward stayed here from time to time. For example, there are three letters from him dated in Newenden on 15 and 17 September 1302, respectively (two on the latter date). It has also been suggested that he may have had a hunting lodge, or even a somewhat more regal building in Newenden. This speculation was first noted by Holloway, who takes as evidence the names of a few fields on the northern side of the ridge, towards Hexden Channel. One of them is called Drawbridge Piece (Drawbridge Marsh), and nearby are Upper and Lower Park Fields, which might be references to some sort of royal mansion – but then again, maybe not. These fields are located on the northern side of the ridge, a fair way from the village centre. I suppose an archaeological dig around there might be able to settle the question, but have found no further documentary evidence of this lodge.

The reason for Edward to have spent time in Newenden could be just friendship. He would certainly have known both the Auchers at Lossenham, and the Waleys's at Newenden (more of them below, p.40ff). It may also have been a convenient base for his close involvement with New Winchelsea.

Old Winchelsea had rapidly become the most important port on the English south coast during the 12th century, but already from 1230, its very existence was threatened by the sea on which it relied for its fortunes. Great storms during the middle of the 13th century continued undermining the town on its gravel bank, to the extent that, by 1280, it was clear that it would sooner or later be doomed to extinction. Plans were then put in place to build a new town on the nearby Iham hill so that, when the 1287 storm sounded the final knell for Old Winchelsea, the burghers had mostly already moved to the new town.

This shows the importance of Winchelsea to the then English economy, and also Edward's preparedness not to let old grievances stand in the way of pragmatic action for the good of the country. Winchelsea had sided with the Earl of Leicester, Simon de Montfort and the barons during the civil war they waged against Edward's father Henry III and Edward himself.

The Earl was also the King's brother-in-law, as he was married to Henry's sister, called Eleanor like many other royal women of the time. His family came from France where his father had cruelly cleansed the Midi of the heretic Cathars, but he was also closely related to the English and French royal families in various ways, including being a direct descendant of William the Conqueror. The civil war was therefore partly family feud, as well as a struggle about the limits of the King's powers.

In the aftermath of the Battle of Evesham (1265), where the royal party finally prevailed, de Montfort's son (also called

Simon) took refuge in Winchelsea and continued to counsel rebellion[49]. The other Cinque Ports soon fell into line, but Winchelsea remained defiant. When the royalists, led by Edward, finally attacked by land and sea, Simon junior fled and the town eventually had to give up. Much to everybody's surprise, Edward's revenge was mild by mediaeval standards, and he assumed the role of Warden of the Cinque Ports, to assure their continued co-operation[50].

New Winchelsea bears the imprint of the King's design. It is laid out as a *bastide* town, safe on the top of a hill, with a rectangular street pattern[51]. The models for this can be found, in particular, in Gascony, which was the only remaining English province in France after Edward's grandfather John (Lackland) had so spectacularly managed to lose the rest of the Angevin empire. Gascony had been Edward's duchy since it was granted to him when he married Eleanor of Castile on 1 Nov 1254, being fifteen years old (Eleanor was thirteen), and he had spent much time there. Development of the new town started after 1283, when Edward appointed a commission for the task, and continued until 1292.

Edward also used Winchelsea to prepare an invasion fleet for attacking France in the autumn of 1295, although it seems he stayed with Sir William de Etchingham at Udimore on that occasion, rather than at Newenden[52]. Two years later, Edward was in Winchelsea again, this time preparing an expedition to Flanders. On that occasion, he survived a giant leap on horseback. His horse was apparently startled by a windmill and jumped over the ramparts of the town, but it fell on its feet and survived unharmed, as did its royal rider[53].

It was during Edward's time that the present church of St. Peter's Newenden was built, but just when remains unclear. Edward's beloved first wife Eleanor died in 1290 and he then married the French princess Margaret in 1299. Perhaps the new and finer church was a requisite for bringing the young Queen to Newenden?

Finally, we can't leave Edward without a mention of the famous entry in the King's Wardrobe accounts, that is the general household expenditure, which indicates that in March 1301[54], Prince Edward, the King's oldest surviving son (and the first English royal to bear the title Prince of Wales) played a game of *creag* at Newenden. Some – and this includes Wisden Cricketer's Almanack, no less – are inclined to interpret this as the first written mention of the game of cricket. It certainly would be, as there are no reliable sightings of the game until 250 years later.

On the other hand, cricket did originate in the Weald and, although it may not have become a sport for grown-ups until the 1600's, it is generally agreed that it was played by children for centuries before that. So, perhaps Prince Edward, then 17 years old, really did play cricket on a sunny field below the new church of St. Peter's, with the Aucher boys and others from his retinue, including his recent new friend Piers Gaveston, that spring day some 700 years ago.

The Aucher family

The Auchers came to England at the time of the Conquest, and take their name from the town of Angers on the Loire, which was their original seat. Perhaps as a result of English unfamiliarity with the name, it can be found spelled with all kinds of variations: Aucher and FitzAucher being the most common, but Anger, Ancher, Alcher and even Albuger[55] can be found.

The first holder of Lossenham manor in the family was Sir Thomas[56], who was born sometime around 1200. He granted land for a Carmelite priory at Lossenham in 1241 or 1242. The Carmelite order stemmed from a 12th century community of hermits who congregated at the well of Elijah on Mt. Carmel, above the modern city of Haifa. By 1226, they gained papal approval as a holy order, but the Sultan's expansion into the Holy Land soon forced them to leave Carmel. They then came to England, and established themselves first at Aylesford, and next at Lossenham. Their sixth General was called Simon Stock, and he is said to have hailed from the Weald (*Stock* means tree trunk, a hollow one being said to have been St Simon's abode at one time). He died in 1265 (allegedly 100 years old) and was promptly canonised. Perhaps it was St Simon's connection with this area that caused the first priories to be established here.

There may be a connection with Edward, too. He had been on a crusade in 1270–71 to the Holy Land, where he was based at Acre, which is just across the bay from Mt. Carmel. Once back in England, he may have been curious to meet with English Carmelites, especially those that had started out from the original community – some of whom may still have been around at Lossenham.

On 25 November 1275 Edward I had to instruct

> Master R. de Freningham to enquire into the trespass committed by persons unknown in burning the church and houses of the Carmelite friars at Lesseham, near Newenden, and the sheriffs of Sussex and Kent are to provide a jury.[57]

Unfortunately, I can find no information of the outcome of this enquiry.

The priory was eventually disestablished during the Reformation; there was little wealth to be found, "the house was poor in building, had no lead but only tile, and much of it was ready to fall[58]" and the buildings were razed to the ground. No doubt the better pieces of stone ended up in subsequent village houses – today there are no traces left of the priory, except in the names of fields and properties around Lossenham.

Sir Thomas's son Henry fought with Edward against the Scots and was made a Knight Banneret (a superior kind of knight) at the battle of Caerlaverock in 1300. Sir Henry would certainly have been on friendly terms with Edward, and he was most likely the host for the King's visits to Newenden at that time.

Henry's oldest son was called Thomas and was knighted at some point. His younger brother Peter was a favourite of Edward II – which was not always a good thing to be. Sir Thomas had a son called Nicholas who was a Gentleman of the King's chamber in 1313.

One Isabel or Isabella Aucher (presumably a widow, since she was able to make decisions of magnitude herself, and in that case perhaps she had been married to this Nicholas – the timing would be about right) built the Knelle Wall, together with her neighbour on the other side of the Rother.

Eventually, the manor was inherited by Anne Aucher who brought it in marriage to the Culpeper family around 1500, and after that, the Aucher family is no longer associated with Newenden.

The Waleys family

There are two branches of the Waleys family with some relevance to the history of Newenden. The name is just a latinised way of writing "Welsh", but it might also mean "the foreigner" – it stems from the word *wilisc*, simply meaning "stranger" in Anglo-Saxon.

On the one hand we have Henry le Waleys, who was a wealthy Londoner, appointed by Edward in 1283 to the commission for re-building Winchelsea[59]. He had held the post of Mayor of Bordeaux at one stage, and was well acquainted with the *bastide* style of towns (see above). He was a trusted servant of Edward's and had served as Mayor of London both at the time of Edward's coronation, and again in 1281 at the King's direct wish, in order to consolidate the royal hold on the city[60].

On the other hand, we have the Waleys family at Glynde Place near Lewes. I am not sure how they were related to Henry, if at all – it may have been a reasonably common surname. The Glynde Place archives are held at the East Sussex Record Office in Lewes and are a rich source of information about that manor and the families that held it[61]. The Waleys's also held Newenden from the archbishop, at least from the late 12th century onwards. Apart from Glynde and Newenden, their empire included West Tarring and Patching in Sussex, and Thanington in Kent.

The first known Waleys holder of Newenden manor was Richard le Waleys (I), who was active around 1180–1200. His widow Denise then held the manor, but when she re-married around 1210, she passed it on to her son Godfrey le Waleys. His son Godfrey (II) inherited it in 1237, and then his son Richard (II) in turn after Godfrey's death in 1266.

This Richard seems to have been a particularly cantankerous and difficult character. In 1276 he was ordered to release the manor of West Tarring, because he had mistreated his tenants and also he had committed the grave crime of spending a mere £6.17s.5¾d. on food at one of Archbishop Robert Kilwardby's visits. At the same time, he also had to relinquish his "right of chase" in the archiepiscopal manors of South Malling and Mayfield.

He made trouble in Newenden, too. According to the Hundred Rolls, a review into the rights of manors in Kent dating from 1274[62], the jury for Newenden township said

> that Richard le Walays takes toll from barges and from small boats, that is 6d. for 1 penny [in other words, he had

been overcharging by 500%] to be paid on the occasion and this unjustly for 15 years. Then they say that the same lord Richard of Newenden claims to have a gallows, the assize of bread and ale and this through the liberty of the archbishop as they understand and he holds this throughout his time and the time of his ancestors.

The rights to have a gallows and the assize of bread and ale were additional, beyond those granted to the lord of the manor as a matter of course. Whether they had been properly granted by the Archbishop as overlord, or just assumed by Richard is hard to say.

According to the Glynde Place archives, the men of Rye became so incensed at the tolls Richard was charging at Newenden, that in 1281 they distrained on [i.e., confiscated the goods of] his tenants in revenge.

There is also a letter held in the National Archives[63] from the barons of Winchelsea to Edward I, concerning a dispute over manorial income involving Richard and his overlord, the Archbishop. It has not been transcribed and translated before, but with kind help from specialists in mediaeval writing and Latin I can now present the following interpretation:

To our most noble Lord, venerable and more highly esteemed than others, our Lord Edward, by the grace of God the most illustrious King of England, Lord of Ireland and Duke of Aquitania, his Barons of the port of Winchelsea [send] their greetings and [express] their readiness [to perform] anything that he wishes.

Since the people of Lord Richard le Waleys, in the township of Newenden, which he holds for His Lordship the Archbishop of Canterbury / - - - / belong to you and during the time of your ancestors, Kings of England, have always been yours, administrated through the authority [?] of the aforementioned Lord Richard le Waleys, [in spite of these circumstances] the aforementioned Lord

Archbishop, wishing that your customary rights, through which the fixed payment of your town of Winchelsea together with other customary rights and other income there ought to be collected through your bailiffs and ought to be paid to you, [wishing that these customary rights] ought to be abolished and annihilated, has sent his / - - - / and commanding letter to his Lordship the Archdeacon of Lewes or his / - - - / in order that he should communicate [?] the state [??] of your town of Rye and force your bailiffs to dismiss and give up the aforementioned customary rights of yours, [threatening] constantly with his verdict of excommunication and interdict [if this is not done].

These customary rights do not concern us, unless bailiffs are appointed by you in order to collect them. And if it so pleases you to forsake these rights in the interest of the aforementioned Lord Archbishop or his people, may your wish then be fulfilled, in these matters as in others. But if not, you may do as you want according to your wishes concerning the question mentioned here. And protect us, if it pleases you, from being troubled in the future for the reason mentioned above.

May your Excellency be healthy and prosper for a very long time.

Although there are some words missing because they are illegible (indicated above with / - - - /) it seems quite clear that the Barons of Winchelsea were having a major argument with the Archbishop. The letter is not dated, but must be from the late 13th century; the Archbishop is either John Peckham or Robert Winchelsey. Unfortunately, it doesn't quite make sense.

At first glance, the dispute seems to concern feudal rents from Winchelsea, but it would not have been paying any such rents – it was a Cinque Port and therefore free of overlords and their imposts. There might have been some duties on trade, but Edward abolished those for the Cinque Ports in the course of his reign.

It is even harder to understand what the Archbishop would have had to do with any dispute over rents or other income from Winchelsea. He would certainly not have had any rights to income from a Cinque Port and it seems highly unlikely he would have tried to claim any such right. Edward and the Archbishops carried on a constant battle over money, but this concerned the taxation of the clergy, which is not mentioned in the letter. The mention of Richard le Waleys also seems out of place in this context – he was just a minor lord with no known Winchelsea connection.

The National Archives describe this document as being a dispute between the Barons and the Archbishop over revenue from Newenden, and I think that is the most probable interpretation. It is likely that the words on the second line of the previous page: "fixed payment of ... Winchelsea" refer to moneys due to Winchelsea, rather than from the town. Perhaps some of the missing words would clarify this.

The document then makes some sense. The King was of course the ultimate overlord of all manors, but Canterbury had been granted the manor of Newenden by a monarch before 1066. The Archbishop had then put the Waleys's in as lords of the manor. It is entirely conceivable that Edward I had decided to take the manor back, or at least to confiscate its rents, perhaps because he needed them for the re-building of Winchelsea. That would certainly annoy the Archbishop and make him threaten excommunication and interdict.

The Barons of Winchelsea, however, say "These customary rights do not concern us". Maybe they were just pointing out that they did not want to get involved in a dispute over feudal rights, as long as they could have the money?

This letter and its background certainly demand further research.

In any event, Sir Richard was obviously not a popular person in the area. He did, however, marry Joan, daughter of Thomas Gates of Newenden, by whom he had two sons, Richard (III) and Godfrey (III). Richard (II) died around 1300 and Joan then re-married. As a result of her new marriage, she became involved in a famous case of English common law (*Petstede v. Marreys*, 1310) which helped establish the rules of trespass[64].

Richard (III) fought with Edward I in Scotland in 1297, 1298 and 1301 but (or perhaps therefore) died without children, so his brother inherited the manors. He, too, fought in Scotland, notably at Bannockburn in 1314.

Godfrey had four sons resulting from two marriages: John, William, Thomas and Godfrey. Both John and William appear to have been High Sheriffs of Surrey and Sussex, John in 1365 and William in 1383. John is said to have been 100 years old when he died in 1375. It was presumably a son or nephew who was that John from whom Richard II removed Newenden fair, see above (p.21) in the discussion about the market.

Perhaps not surprisingly, there was a big dispute over the inheritance after Godfrey's death. The estate was finally distributed in 1440, but there are apparently no records to show what happened to the Newenden manor, and so the family disappears from the scope of our history.

Population

Of course, the ordinary people of Newenden have left far fewer marks in history than the nobles from its heyday. But that does not mean there are no traces of them. In particular, there is a great deal of evidence of taxation starting from the late 13th century. The National Archives in Kew hold at least 17 records of taxation rolls from Newenden, showing charges from various years between 1300 and 1500[65]. These include the names of people who were liable to pay taxes and the basis on which they were taxed. Unfortunately, few of the records have been transcribed, yet.

The very first record of this nature is of course Domesday Book. For Newenden, it shows 29 villagers and smallholders (for the text, see note 20). This count only reflects the adult free men in the village, so it seems reasonable to think that there may have been around 100–150 people living here then.

The next transcribed tax record of relevance to Newenden is the Kent Lay Subsidy of 1334[66], which was first published in translation in 1961[67]. Helpfully, the editors made a special comparison between the results for Newenden township in this roll and the following taxation in 1338, noting that in 1334, there were eleven taxpayers, paying a total of £1.13s.11d., but in 1338, there were twelve, now paying £1.14s.11d., with the newcomer assessed at 1 shilling. There were, however, detail changes to the amounts payable by the others, so clearly the taxation took note of the changing financial fortunes of the villagers[68].

It is difficult to say how many people these eleven or twelve taxpayers represent in total. Not all householders were liable to tax, as they had to have a certain minimum wealth before they were taxed. The suggestion is that less than 50% of the households were taxed, so there may have been around 25 households – a similar figure to that 250 years earlier. Again, therefore, the total population would have been between 100 and 150.

By comparison, the rest of Selbrittenden hundred, including Lossenham, Sandhurst and parts of Hawkhurst and Benenden, contained 32 householders liable to tax, paying a total of £3.10s.7½d. It is interesting to see that Isabel Aucher, the powerful lady of Lossenham, was the wealthiest of those 32, being liable for 10 shillings.

Shortly after this assessment, the Black Death reached England (from 1348) and, in the Marshes, this led to drastic falls in the population and wholesale abandonment of settlements[69]. However, there is no specific evidence of the impact it may have had on Newenden. Perhaps a study of the later taxation records could provide a clue here.

From 1559, we are fortunate enough to have transcriptions of the church registers of baptisms, marriages and burials. With the Reformation came a requirement on parish churches to keep these records and Newenden has almost complete records, transcribed by the Rev. Edmund Jermyn at the end of the 19th century. Based on these, we can guess the number of parishioners and in particular, we can see the population changes over the years. In my view, the villagers at the beginning of the period, around 1560, may have numbered just under 150; rapidly rising to 200 in about 1620; and then equally rapidly falling below 100 in 1640; reaching an absolute bottom in the early 18th century at about 50 and then climbing back above 100 around 1800.

It is striking how, for almost all the years before 1730 or so, the number of burials exceeds the number of baptisms. This to my mind is an indication that the village was to a great extent populated by labourers who came here to work and perhaps died young, not least from malaria. This was a notorious problem in the Marshes until, in the latter half of the 18th century, the drainage systems improved and the malaria-carrying mosquitoes could be kept at bay. The situation is very similar in other parishes in the Marshes, too, with burials nearly double the number of baptisms at times, and following the same time-scale as that noted for Newenden[70].

I would think the big increase at the beginning of the 17th century was related to an influx of labour for the ultimately unsuccessful works on taming the Rother at that time. The decline after that attempt was given up is probably a reflection of the decline of Rye, whose port was now seriously silting up. By 1600, its population was down to 2,000 from a peak of 5,000 just fifty years before. Newenden, being increasingly dependent for its business on acting as a feeder of traffic through Rye, was naturally suffering along with the main port.

In 1662, after the Restoration, a new tax was introduced to support the Royal Household. It was payable at 1 shilling per hearth in the taxable households, due at Michaelmas (29 September) and Lady Day (25 March). Inevitably, it became known as the Hearth Tax, or sometimes the Chimney Tax. (It was repealed after the Glorious Revolution in 1688/9.)

The Kent taxation rolls for the Hearth Tax from Lady Day 1664 have been published[71] and show, for the township of Newenden, 17 householders and 4 exempt. In the rest of Selbrittenden hundred, there were 35 householders, of which perhaps one was in Newenden parish outside the township. It was not a popular tax, and it is noted for John Pellatt and Thomas Welsted that each "refuseth to make any account of his fire hearthes".

Our next source of information about the actual number of households in Newenden comes from the Land Tax assessments 1780–1832[72]. From these we can see that, at the start of the period, there were nine landowners in the township. The biggest was Samuel Bishop, accounting for land assessed at £69 (including "Frogs Barn Farm", which he held as tenant) out of the total £179. Perhaps surprisingly, the second biggest landowner was the Rev. Thomas Morphett, who was Rector of Newenden at the time.

When Hasted wrote his history of Kent, just at the end of the 18th century, he says there were only 15 houses in the parish, and by 1832, there appear to have been no more than eleven in the township.

For 1841, we have a detailed picture of the land and its ownership, in the form of the Tithe Awards[73], for which a completely new survey was made of all property in the parish. This was called for by the Tithe Commutation Act of 1836, which had been long in preparation and negotiation. It meant the end of the old taxation system whereby (originally), a tenth of all produce of the land was payable (in kind) to the rector of the parish. But the system had become increasingly unwieldy and in many cases, tithes had been commuted to cash payments, or converted to a fixed sum payable once and for all. It was time to introduce a new, cash-based system, and so all parishes were surveyed and their properties listed. Newenden is particularly lucky in having had a very detailed and precise survey carried out. There were now 25 landowners listed, holding a total of 1,046 acres divided over 203 distinct property units, worth a total (in annual income) of £238.18s.3d. Of the land area, 743 acres (nearly three-quarters) was pasture, with 193 acres of arable land and 45 acres of hops – the miracle crop of the time.

After this, we have the Census records from Newenden, showing the population hovering around 150 until the middle of the 20th century – but then we are no longer in the realm of Early Newenden.

Families of Newenden

The transcribed church registers of Newenden (see above p.49) provide a means of identifying individual villagers and their families through the centuries. It is notable how few families seem to have stayed here for more than one or two generations. This is another sign of how the population, at least in the bad years between 1550 and 1750, mostly consisted of relatively transient labourers.

A few early names stand out. There was a family called A'Rye (that is, "of Rye") which seems to have lived here in two instalments, or perhaps it was just two different families moving here from Rye. The first was John A'Rye, who married a Newenden girl called Joan Woodland in April 1564. He seems to have been a belligerent sort of fellow, for there is a memorandum to the Mayor of Rye from July 1575[74], stating:

> One John of Rye dwelling at Newenden, Thomas Rofe of Rye and Thomas Wood of Rye, Robert Collyer of Tenterden and Roger Morris dwelling in Sussex upon Thursday sennight[75], being the 21th daye of this moneth, assembled themselves together, as I am enformed, in the Parishe of Stone in the Ile of Oxney, and there the said John of Rye was named by the others to be their Capitayne, and the said Thomas Rofe his Sargent, and the others to be his soldyers and the said John of Rye requyred dyvers of the inhabitants within the said Ile to be sworne to hym to be his soldiers and suche as refused to doo, he abused with threatninge woordes and otherwise.

He was relatively wealthy, having servants – two of whom died while in service... (1568 and 1580). He was himself buried at Newenden on 30 May 1583.

The second A'Rye family to have lived in Newenden was started when Henry married Martha Cutbush, who was of a relatively large Newenden family, in March 1656. They had at least one child, and Henry also had one child recorded from a previous marriage. He died in October 1660 and Martha in October 1671.

The Cutbushes can be traced from one Edward, who married Mary Petter in July 1639, but he had previously been married to a Martha, who was the mother of Martha A'Rye mentioned above. Edward and Martha's first child was called Mary; she was baptised on 30 August 1618 and buried on 1 January 1658.

A grandson (probably – I can't quite trace the connection) of Edward Cutbush was called Thomas. This man had at least three children of which the middle, a son also called Thomas, was baptised on 31 January 1657 and buried on 9 April 1714. He had seven children noted in the registers, two of whom were called Thomas (the first son died just two years old and, as was common practice, the next son to be born in the family was given the same name). The surviving Thomas married Ann Catt on 3 September 1706 and they had at least two children. The last mention of a Cutbush in Newenden is, inevitably, a Thomas, who was buried on 20 April 1812, but there is a gap during the 18th century when there are no mentions of this family and its members in the registers.

Other families with frequent entries include the Igglesdens, the Levetts, the Sisleys and the Hanson family, landlords at the White Hart from the late 18th century until the middle of the 19th.

Undoubtedly the most widely connected and presumably also wealthiest family in the village was that of the Bishops.

They came from Cranbrook and it appears to have been a Nicholas, who was born in October 1672, who first moved here. He bought Lossenham in 1702 and died in April 1733, probably childless. He was one of six siblings. The oldest was Peter, who married Anne Clarke in June 1697 in Lewes and had at least two daughters; the older, Sarah, was baptised in Newenden on 6 August 1699. Sarah married (in June 1722[76]) Thomas Frewen of Brickwall in Northiam, which gave later Bishop family members a useful family connection to the wealthy and influential Frewens.

This Thomas Frewen was a medical doctor, famous for being one of the first to introduce inoculation against smallpox, and also wrote scientific works on the treatment of smallpox and other diseases. He was a descendant of John Frewen, a Puritan who became Rector of Northiam in 1583. John's oldest son, Accepted Frewen, became Archbishop of York in 1660, while his fourth son Stephen bought the Brickwall estate in 1666, where the family continued to reside until it was converted into a school.

Another brother of Nicholas Bishop was Thomas, who was buried in Newenden on 14 February 1746. He was married twice and had at least seven children, of whom Samuel was the youngest, but Lossenham nonetheless was inherited by this Samuel. He was baptised in February 1725 and married Mary Plaine, who died on 3 May 1800, having had ten children, most of whom survived infancy and had families of their own.

Samuel leased "Newenden ffarme" from Thomas Frewen – his uncle by marriage – for 21 years from Lady Day 1755[77]. This property, which is referred to as Frogs Barn Farm in the tithe award schedules, contained one barn, three lodges and about 110 acres of land, with marl-pits and ponds – there is particular mention in the lease that "Mr Bishop is to repair the ponds and fences".

Samuel's and Mary's fifth child was Samuel junior, who was baptised on 2 May 1755 and married Elizabeth, who was born in 1758. Being the oldest surviving son, he inherited the Lossenham estate when his father died in December 1814, nearly 90 years old. They had no children, and Samuel in his will bequeathed a sum of money for the education of the children of Newenden. This first resulted in the setting up of Newenden School, which was in operation from the 1850's (Elizabeth died in March 1851) until 1930. The income from the bequest is now distributed by the Samuel Bishop Foundation as grants to village children in secondary schools.

Samuel Jr's oldest sister Sarah was baptised on 2 October 1748. She married Thomas Ayerst from Hawkhurst on 14 August 1770 and they lived in Newenden, where they had five children. Sarah died on 12 June 1789 and she is remembered on a wall memorial in black stone on the south wall inside the church.

The oldest Ayerst child was named Thomas and he became a coal and timber merchant, operating at Newenden Wharf. He was born in 1773, married Elizabeth Russell from Rye in 1797 and died on 4 March 1855. They had two sons and three daughters. The sons were called Thomas and Samuel, and both were coal merchants, Thomas staying in Newenden with the family business and Samuel moving elsewhere. Thomas (III) married a Northiam girl called Louisa Goble, whose uncle William was married to Priscilla Bishop, who was the sixth of Samuel senior's ten children (so Thomas and Louisa were, if I am right, first cousins once removed).

To finish the family chronicles, reflect a moment on the inscription on the gravestone (in Newenden churchyard) of Thomas' and Louisa's third child, Samuel, who died aged 23 in September 1857: "There was hope in this young man's end".

Manors, Township and Liberty

Manors

The concept of a feudal manor is that of an estate with defined boundaries, with a lord to whom rents are paid, and to whom work and goods may have to be delivered by the tenants. After the Conquest, this system became formalised and set up a class of lords of the manor, as against all the rest, who were mere tenants or worse and had little chance to rise to the manor-holding class. But even before the Normans introduced full-on feudalism, manors had started to coalesce for each major settlement, as a convenient unit of administration[78].

There always was an idea in English law that the King was the ultimate holder of all land, so the very earliest manors were all held by the King and the tenants paid their dues, in cash and in kind, directly to the Crown. Then the kings decided that giving away the lordship of a manor or two could be a good way of rewarding particularly deserving people. Occasionally the King felt in need of some spiritual assurance, so then he would grant some manors to the Church. Originally, the lord of a manor could decide to divide the manor, perhaps to reward several sons, or a particularly faithful officer. However, in 1290 Edward I introduced the Act of *Quia Emptores*, which stopped this practice and effectively settled the number of manors in England for the future.

The core of the manorial rights was the right to receive rents for land used by the tenants – the *villeins*, to use the mediaeval terminology – and to hold a manorial court to act as a court of first instance for many crimes and breaches of the local regulations, known as "the custom of the manor". In addition to this, the lord of the manor might be granted further rights and the lords of Newenden manor in particular claimed a number of such rights.

From the Hundred Rolls (discussed in the section on the Waleys family, p.43f) we have seen that Richard le Waleys claimed the right of having a gallows as well as the assize of bread and ale. In other records, it appears that Newenden manor also came with a pillory and with the right of *infangenthef*, that is the right to try thieves caught red-handed on the manor's land. (The complementary right of *outfangenthef* – this applies to thieves caught outside the manor – is not mentioned, however.) These rights seem particularly appropriate to a manor deriving its role from a weekly market.

There were two manors locally: Lossenham, which was in the hand of the King, and Newenden, whose overlord was the Archbishop of Canterbury[79]. It is not known who granted Newenden manor to the Archbishop, but it must have been a king before the Conquest – unfortunately, the charter by which this was done has not survived. It may well have been Edward the Confessor, as he was particularly generous in giving manors to the Church.

It is interesting to note that, even though there are two manors, there is only one parish of Newenden, which covers both manors. Most parishes were founded by the lord of the manor, and the parish therefore by definition catered for the same area as the manor itself. But before this became the general practice, some parishes were created as offspring of a head minster[80]. It is therefore possible that the reference in the *Domesday Monachorum* to a St. Peter's church belonging to Lyminge (of which more below, p.64) is to Newenden parish, and that the church was just such a daughter establishment from Lyminge. It might even have been created before Newenden was split off from Lossenham, which would make the parish very old indeed. So far as I can tell, there has never been a church at Lossenham – except of course for that belonging to the Carmelite priory, but that was for the friars themselves, not a parish church for the laity.

Lossenham manor was held by the Aucher family[81], as discussed before in connection with Edward I. When the manor finally passed to a daughter, Anne, who was born around 1480, she carried Lossenham with her in marriage to Walter Culpeper, and it then stayed in the Culpeper family until 1628, when it was sold to a Surrey gentleman called Adrian Moore[82]. His heirs then sold the manor to Nicholas Bishop in 1702 – he was the first of the Bishop family to move to Lossenham and was, I think, the great-uncle of Samuel Bishop of Foundation fame.

Domesday Book states that Newenden belongs to the Archbishop and refers to the rent from the manor in the time of Edward the Confessor (i.e. before 1066). In a precursor to Domesday Book, the Archbishop's reply to the inquiry states that Newenden was held by a certain Leofric[83] in those days[84]. At some point in the 12th century, he granted it to the Waleys family, who continued to hold it until about 1440[85]. It is then unclear how it was held, until 1542, when Thomas Cranmer, the then Archbishop of Canterbury, gave it back to the King – Henry VIII.

This, incidentally, was a difficult time for Cranmer. In February 1542, Henry's fifth wife, Catherine Howard, had been executed for adultery, following an investigation started by Cranmer. As the bearer of the bad news about Catherine's infidelity, Cranmer's status with the King must have been affected in unpredictable ways, which will have been dangerous for a man so dependent on royal support against his many enemies. From a Newenden point of view, a further intriguing detail is that the Queen's alleged lover was Thomas Culpeper, one of Henry's courtiers. He was very closely related to the Lossenham Culpepers – his father Sir Alexander was the older brother of that Walter who married Anne Aucher and thus gained the manor of Lossenham.

Newenden manor continued to be held by the monarchs of England until Cromwell decided to shorten Charles I by a head, at which point it was sold to a certain Hugh Peters. At the Restoration, the manor promptly went back to the Crown, where it stayed until at some point in the 18th century, it was conveyed to the Earl of Aylesford (who was a descendant of the Earls of Winchilsea [sic]). The 3rd Earl, just like all the first seven Earls of Aylesford, was called Heneage Finch, and he sold the manor to Samuel Bishop (senior) in 1760[86].

Thus the Bishop family finally managed to unite the two manors.

Hundreds and lathes

When the Kentish people started organising lower levels of government in the ninth century or so, they formed units called "hundreds". These are a common feature for Germanic peoples and typically, a hundred is defined as the area which could support a hundred households, or sometimes the area which could supply a hundred armed men in times of war – this might have been much the same thing. Newenden and Lossenham, together with Sandhurst and smaller parts of what today are the parishes of Benenden and Hawkhurst, belonged to a hundred called Selbrittenden. This may be a distortion of Silverden, in which case the main gathering point for the hundred would have been in the western part of Sandhurst, where there still is a place so called today.

The hundred was the main taxation and judicial unit, and there were around 60 in Kent. Here, law officers of the county met every four weeks to settle any disputes and sentence criminals caught since the last hundred court was held.

Most of England was eventually organised into hundreds, but in Kent only[87], there is also a larger subdivision called "lathes", of which there were originally seven, perhaps reflecting provinces of the old independent Kentish kingdom. Selbrittenden hundred belonged to the lathe of Lympne. Around 1200, the seven lathes were reorganised into five, and Selbrittenden was placed in the new lathe of Scray. It is debatable whether lathes or hundreds are the older institution; however, neither of them play any role today, although neither have been formally abolished.

The township of Newenden

At some point – it seems likely to have been in the 12th century, but certainly before 1227 – the Archbishop requested to have his manor, i.e. Newenden, withdrawn from the jurisdiction of the hundred. A separate entity known as the Township, sometimes called the Liberty (in the sense of being free of the hundred duties), of Newenden was formed. It covered most of the present village, south of Frogs Hill Lane and north of the river, and also about a field's width to the east of Lossenham Lane, but not Lossenham itself – that was a separate manor and remained within the hundred.

The effect of this was to give the Township its own administration. This was provided by two officers called the Bailiff and the Under-bailiff. It also meant that the Township could hold its own court, which probably was the reason for this arrangement. In a village with an important market, especially one bordering on the next county (which had different laws and customs) it would be desirable to dispense justice quickly, while the malfeasors were still around. This also added to the prestige of the market and the village, and naturally to that of the Lord of the manor, who presided over the court.

Beresford and Finberg list Newenden as a borough in 1227, one of only eleven in Kent at the time, as it was "[r]epresented as a hundred, borough or vill by its own jury at the eyre". Although mediaeval boroughs normally were far more urban settlements than Newenden can have been, "burghality" (as the authors call it) might be achieved through royal charter, but it could also be thrust upon a village for taxation or juridical reasons[88]. Clearly Newenden belongs to the juridical group of boroughs, as a result of being a township. The Eyre Rolls list the records of enquiries into the rights and privileges held in various locations. These required a number of jurors to be selected from each administrative unit, and they then had to report under oath what the local situation was. Newenden always had its own jury, and was reported separately from the rest of Selbrittenden in the proceedings. It would appear that the first occasion documented was in 1227. A further review of these Rolls might be worthwhile.

It is interestingly contradictory that Hasted says that, in the 21st year of Edward I's reign (1293), Archbishop Boniface unsuccessfully claimed exemption for his tenants from serving at the Hundred Court, and from associated taxes. A slight problem is that Boniface of Savoy died in 1270, so there must be a mistake somewhere. But perhaps the obligation to attend the Hundred Court remained, even after the Township had been established – the evidence is quite clear that by that time, the Liberty of Newenden was in full force.

The Township and Liberty of Newenden continued until 1866, when the Poor Law Amendment Act abolished all townships and other areas that levied a separate rate, and made them all civil parishes, which were governed by vestry meetings. At this point, the delineation between ecclesiastical and civil parishes was not completely clear, and the vestry meetings appear to have been run by a Chairman, the churchwarden and two Overseers of the Poor. The post of Overseer was a very old one and there is a note in the Church-wardens' accounts[89] from 1688 that Monday of Easter week is the day for electing Churchwardens and Overseers.

The civil parishes were then revised and more strictly formalised through the Local Government Act 1894, which determined that all parishes with more than 300 electors should elect a Parish Council. Smaller parishes would instead hold semi-annual parish meetings.

The 1894 Act also banned parish meetings from being held at licensed premises. In Newenden, the vestry meetings had been held at the White Hart. On 12 July 1883, the vestry meeting minuted:

> It was unanimously resolved that in consequence of the increased expenses incurred by the Highway Board of the District of Tenterden and the inequality [should that be inequity, I wonder?] of the charges it is desirable that such Board be dissolved[90].

One wonders if perhaps the ban on meetings in the pub might have been quite a good idea...

On 4 December 1894, the minutes of the vestry meeting include:

> The unanimous feeling of the meeting was that no application should be made to the County Council for powers to elect a Parish Council by being grouped with another Parish.

It wasn't until 1962 that the typically independence-minded Newenden electors agreed to form a Parish Council, by which time changes of the law permitted even small parishes to elect such councils.

Church

St. Peter's Church in Newenden was probably built around 1300, or perhaps a little earlier. There may have been an older church building here before that time, indeed it is likely there was, as Newenden was a moderately important trading and market venue, but we know nothing for certain about any previous church.

There exists a collection of manuscripts known as the *Domesday Monachorum* (the Domesday Book of the monks), which contains various records of churches and the properties of Canterbury, dating from about 1087[91]. One of those manuscripts lists churches which belong to other churches (in some sense which is not entirely clear, but possibly because they were daughter establishments of the main church). In here, under churches belonging to Lyminge, we find one St. Peter's church – no location is given – and this may be a reference to Newenden, as the neighbouring parish church of Wittersham is also counted in this group, together with Stanford, [Monks] Horton, Stowting, Bircholt, Stelling, Acrise, Paddlesworth and one St. Martin's Church, again without location[92]. It is rather a disparate group, and St. Peter's Church in Molash would seem to have at least an equal claim to being the church referred to in this document.

Note also that there is no mention of any parish church in Newenden in its Domesday Book entry, nor elsewhere in contemporaneous listings of Kent churches, whereas all those churches shown above as belonging to Lyminge can be found in their respective entries (except for Wittersham, Stanford and Bircholt, which are not shown as separate manors in Domesday Book). However, this might be because Newenden church was not the property of the manor, which could indicate that it had been founded significantly earlier – see the discussion above re manors, p.57f.

Domesday Book lists churches when they are part of the manor, but in many cases no church is mentioned, even for large settlements which almost certainly did have one or more churches. This is an indication that the local church was older than the manor. Examples in Kent include Lenham, Sandwich, Darenth, Bromley and Charing (among many more), so Newenden may be in good company.

The earliest certain mention of a church in Newenden is in a letter of 6 January 1272[93], where the Prior of Dover St. Martin refers to his nephew Richard, rector of Newenden Church. In 1288, Pope Nicholas IV granted the tenths (that is, the tithes which would normally go to the Church) to King Edward I for six years, in support of a planned expedition to the Holy Land. A taxation by the King's Precept was begun in that year and finished accounting for the domains of Canterbury arch-diocese in 1291. In this document[94], we can find a reference to *Ecclesia de Newenden*", which was assessed at £9.6s.8d. So there was definitely a church here then, but whether that was the present building or an older one is not possible to say.

Even at a cursory glance, it is evident that the church building as it looks now has been much changed over the centuries. (See outline plan p.86.) The chancel and small turret on the south-west corner are recent additions, of which

more later. The nave of the church is clearly shorter than it
once was. If you look to the north, you will see that the
eastern-most arch is broken and ends in the wall to the
chancel, without the expected pillar support. When the
modern chancel was built in 1930–31, the foot of the missing
pillar was found and this has been preserved in a niche on the
outside of the church. If you look to the south, you will notice
two arches (the western filled in). These are, curiously, wider
than their counterparts on the north side. If you imagine
three arches on the south side, and four on the north side,
both sides would be approximately equal, and one might
hazard a guess that was the original length of the nave.

Looking now at the aisles, you can tell that these were once
wider – much wider in the case of the south aisle, where you
can just about see the left third or so of a transversal arch at
the eastern end. In my view, the church originally had equally
wide aisles, about three times as wide as the south aisle is
now. Each of the aisles had its own roof, as did the nave, so
that there were three distinct ridges to the overall roof.

After the Black Death and other troubles of the 14th century,
the church was probably too big for the population, especially
if the market was no longer attracting crowds. Also, one
might guess that the valleys between the roof ridges were
prone to leaking. So, at some point perhaps in the 15th century,
the decision was taken to make the aisles narrower so the
whole building could be covered by a single roof. The king
post construction of the present roof dates from that time.

There are a couple of wills from the 16th century[95] which
provide for money to be given for the Lady Chapel in the
parish church of Newenden. A Lady Chapel is a small side
chapel in a church, dedicated to the Virgin Mary. It is
interesting, and indicative of a larger building, that St. Peter's
still had such a chapel then.

In March 1700 (or so, the letter[96] is undated), the parish-ioners, together with Rectors of surrounding parishes, wrote to the Archbishop to say the following:

> That the Steeple of the said Parish Church of Newenden being several years ago very much damaged by lightning and soon after fell down, & together with it the Chancel, there being one wall common to both; so that both Steeple & Chancel have for six or seven years lain in a ruinous heap to the great grief of the Petitioners, several of which are so poor that it might prove the utter undoing of them to repair the same, the Parish being so very small, & the body of the Church which is standing (tho much out of repair) is more than enough to contain the in-habitants & to perform all Offices of Divine Worship decently in.

They asked for, and were granted, permission to pull down what remained of the "Steeple & Chancel" and rebuild the church to be more suitable for the much reduced population. Now the interesting thing about this is the part which says *there being one wall common to both*. It seems to me that the only way there could have been a common wall between the tower and the chancel is if the tower was in a central position, between the nave and the chancel. Most churches, especially small ones, have their tower at the western end; and the chancel is always at the eastern end. But there is no other way of interpreting this letter, and it was written and signed by a number of distinctly reputable people (such as the rectors of neighbouring parishes, as well as Thomas Fishenden, the then Rector of Newenden).

There are not many churches with a central tower in the Canterbury diocese, at least not small ones. But looking beyond the border, St. Michael's Church in Playden is an almost perfect example of what St. Peter's might have looked like. It is slightly older, but the style is unmistakably the same. Interestingly, St. Peter's Church may well have been built at the time when King Edward was engaged in the re-building of Winchelsea at its current location on Iham hill, so he and his retinue would have been riding past Playden on their way to and from Winchelsea, assuming they were stay-ing at Newenden.

It is remarkable that lightning alone could have caused the structure to be so damaged that it fell down, but it was not an altogether uncommon fate for churches in the days before the lightning conductor was invented. The church tower was usu-ally the tallest structure in the vicinity and so would be prone to lightning strikes, which can have enormous force. Of course, it doesn't help that the church stands on a hill of unstable clay and the foundations were presumably very sketchy (as they were for all buildings of the time).

In 1700, then, the ruins of the Steeple & Chancel were pulled down and taken away at a cost of £15, as evidenced by the accounts of the churchwardens[97]. The following year, the east wall of the church was re-constructed where the opening to the modern chancel is today; and a new, square tower was built on the north-west corner of the church. The total cost of these works came to £57.14s.3d., of which £5.17s.4d. was the fee for the permission to do so (!).

The decision was then taken to arrange the interior somewhat unorthodoxly, with the pews facing south and the altar by the south wall, where the wooden screen now provides some delineation for the vestry.

The screen has shields of arms along the top, which represent people in some way connected with the village. The first and third position from the left are blank. The second contains the arms of Eleanor of Castile, Edward I's first spouse, although unusually, the arms of Castile and Leon are shown quartered. The fourth represents the Aucher family, the fifth the Culpepers. Then the arms of the Diocese of

Canterbury and in the seventh position, we find the arms of the St. Leger family, which the Auchers were entitled to display after Henry Aucher married Joan St. Leger sometime around 1400[98]. Next the royal arms of Edward III, the first English king to lay claim to the French throne as well.

I can't identify the eighth shield. It looks similar to the arms usually representing the Bishop family, but that shield has three golden coins on a red background, whereas this has three black trefoils on a silver background[99]. Perhaps the Bishops of Lossenham used this variation? The complex royal arms thereafter are those of the Hanoverian kings of the United Kingdom from 1816 until 1837, so presumably relate to the Royal Arms described below. The following arms belong to the Haydock family, but the connection with Newenden is not obvious. Finally, the royal arms of the monarchs of the United Kingdom from Victoria onwards.

The unusual altar arrangement continued until 1843, when the Archdeacon of Maidstone at his parochial visitation on 14 August ordered

> that the communion table be removed from its present position and placed in the usual place at the east end; also that the Pulpit be removed and placed at the West End of the Church; also that the whole of the present pews be taken down & rearranged ... longitudinally[100].

This Archdeacon seems to have been fond of ordering things to be done. In 1847 he ordered that the Royal Arms of benefaction be removed from the eastern wall and placed on the southern wall. But the villagers took his orders with phlegmatic calm, as these instructions were not carried out until 1852 or so.

These arms, incidentally, represent George IV and were made by a painter called Comport[101]. They now hang at the western end of the north aisle.

Church

By the mid-19th century, the 1701 tower was suffering badly from subsidence, and a consulting architect called Gordon M Hills was brought in to survey the situation and make recommendations. His report[102] was unequivocal:

> The Tower is in a very perilous condition not only itself in imminent danger but threatening a serious injury to the West wall of the church ... The Tower is now seriously fractured from top to bottom in each of its three external walls ... a chasm in the West wall not less than eight inches ... whilst the Whole Tower has gone over 23 inches towards the West..."

The engravings that you can see in some historical notes of Newenden, showing the tower with a big crack, were made for this report, which was issued 20 March 1858.

Hills also recommended that

> in rebuilding the Tower the position should be changed to where the Porch now exists on the south side. At this part of the Church an old arch now stopped up could be reopened to communicate with the Tower; ... for use as a belfry and entrance to the Church.

He also provided a drawing of this design, which was for a much larger tower than the one finally decided upon, which still stands today. This little tower, together with the repairs to the west wall, cost £450, of which £367.5s. were raised by public subscription. Archbishop Sumner himself contributed £10 as did Mr Pomfret, the bank manager at Rye. The Incorporated Church Building Society provided £45, while Mr Frank Morrison of Hole Park gave £25. Other donors included Henry Cazenove, James Dengate at New Barn and finally the servants of Miss L Taylor in Preston, who had herself donated 11 shillings, were pressed to collect 6 shillings for a church few of them would ever see[103].

The present chancel was built in 1930-31 as a memorial to members of the Selmes family and other loved villagers, with contributions from many parishioners of the time. The construction materials match those of the original building very well, as does the roof with its intricate king posts and tie beams. However, it does seem slightly strange that it was decided to make the arches round, as in a Norman church, in contrast to the pointed Early English arches of the nave.

Glebe

This funny old word means non-consecrated land belonging to a parish and used in some way to support the parish priest. Historically, there are two pieces of glebe land in Newenden: the plot where the Old Rectory stands, and the field now used for sheep grazing just off the road to Tenterden. Information about glebe land can be found in documents called "terriers". The oldest Newenden terrier in Canterbury Cathedral Archives is from 30 September 1615[104] and it mentions both pieces of land. There was "a small dwelling house with a barne" for a Rectory, and the Rectory appears to have remained a small and inglorious building until the present house was built towards the end of the 19th century.

The churchwardens' accounts are also preserved from the mid-17th century onwards[105], and they show the income from the field, which was let to farmers. The rent was one pound and five shillings for many years, but it was rebated by four shillings in the 1760's and 1770's. In 1841, the Tithe map shows that the field was used for hops, and indeed it is sometimes referred to as "the Hop Field" even today. These accounts are generally a fascinating source of historical detail. For instance, the parish paid 1 shilling in 1788 for a prayer for the King. By 1811, the tariff for praying for a royal had increased to

1s.6d. and when Prince Albert was being prayed for in 1841, the price was 2 shillings.

The Font

Without doubt, the oldest visible man-made object, as well as the most photographed in the village is the font. It is made from a hard oolitic limestone (stone formed from small concentric, globular grains), which is believed to have been quarried near Sangatte on the French north coast (just where the Channel Tunnel terminates today). The consensus seems to be that it stems from the beginning of the 12th century, but the reality is that nobody really knows.

It is certainly a very interesting artefact. The carvings on three sides carry some form of symbolism but it is not clear what it might be. The most dramatic images are those on the west side, with a wyvern and a lion licking a leaf. The wyvern mostly tends to be associated with the West of England and Wales, but I don't think too many conclusions can be drawn from that. There are also strange beasts, or maybe half-humans, in three of the four roundels on the south side of the font.

There is a copy of the font in St. Mary's church, Rye, but this is a modern replica and not to full scale.

Castle Toll

At the very end of the ridge, just before the levels around the confluence of the Rother and Hexden Channel, stand the earthworks known as Castle Toll. Their origins are as obscure as their name, but there are at least two levels of works; one older in age and larger in area, which is now quite hard to see, except for some edges at the southern end, and one smaller, thought to date from the 13th century and built within the compass of the larger works. This level is still quite clearly visible.

Castle Toll has been archaeologically investigated three times; once in the mid 19th century, and also in 1965 and 1971.

The older works

The older fortification probably enclosed the whole of the extreme end of the peninsula (now, of course, the levels where the waters flowed have been drained and the site looks considerably closer to Hexden Channel than to the Rother). An earth wall, surrounded by a ditch, provided the external defences, and the whole area thus enclosed is about 450m from north to south, and about 200m wide at its widest. The total surface is approximately 16 acres (6.5 ha). However, the works have been badly damaged by agriculture over the centuries[106].

It is not known how old this stronghold might be. The archaeological excavations found no datable remains. It certainly could be pre-Roman and might be the final destination for the ridge-way from Ticehurst to Newenden. It may also have served as a watch-post for the Jutes of Kent against the barbarian South Saxons (see the discussion about the origins of Lossenham, p.14). Older authorities, starting with William Camden, in *Britannia*, have suggested that this might be the site of *Anderida*, a Romano-British fort, later overrun by the Saxons, as described in the Anglo-Saxon Chronicle[107]. Nowadays, it is generally agreed that Pevensey is the correct location for *Anderida*, and since the investigations of Castle Toll have found no evidence at all of Roman or Romano-British occupation, it is hard to make an argument in favour of this theory.

The excavations found a single layer of burnt material, and very little else, indicating that perhaps the fort was never finished, indeed burnt down before fully commissioned. This is interesting because it supports the theory that this older level is the apparently not very impressive fortification destroyed by Vikings in 892.

The Anglo-Saxon Chronicle describes what happened (in translation):

> And they came up with two hundred and fifty ships into the mouth of the Limne, which is in East-Kent, at the east end of the vast wood that we call Andred. This wood is in length, east and west, one hundred and twenty miles, or longer, and thirty miles broad. The river that we before spoke about lieth out of the weald. On this river they towed up their ships as far as the weald, four miles from the mouth outwards; and there destroyed a fort within the

fen, whereon sat a few churls, and which was hastily
wrought.

This hastily wrought fort might well be Castle Toll. It might
also be the "lost" Burghal Hidage strong-point *Eorpeburnan*.
(It is not certain that *Eorpeburnan* was the fort mentioned in
the Chronicle, but there is certainly a good chance – the date,
as well as the location, would be about right.)

The Burghal Hidage is an Old English document listing 33
burhs, or forts[108], which are thought to have been created by
King Alfred in the last quarter of the ninth century to protect
the population of Wessex and southern England against
Viking attacks. Each *burh* is listed in clockwise order around
the coast, together with its "hidage", which is the number of
"hides" which it was supposed to defend. A hide was a unit of
land large enough to support one household, and each household was required to provide one man for the construction,
upkeep, and defence of the *burh*.

All of the 33 sites have been identified, except for the first
one, which is called *Eorpeburnan*. The next one is Hastings,
then follows Lewes, Burpham and so on around Sussex and
Wessex. Since the burhs are spaced relatively evenly, we can
conclude that *Eorpeburnan* must have been somewhere in
the vicinity of Newenden.

The two other candidates mentioned are Rye and Burgh
Hill overlooking the Rother near Etchingham, but even Rye
historians now seem to favour the older Castle Toll site[109].
Burgh Hill is too far inland; the Chronicle says that the fort
was "four miles from the mouth [of the river] *outwards*" (*.iiii.
mila fram ðam muþan uteweardan*) which, if the river emptied into an estuary at Bodiam, would be about right for
Castle Toll.

Eorp or *earp* means dark, and *burna* is a stream (as indeed a
burn still is in Scotland), so *Eorpeburnan* means the dark

stream – quite suitable for a site next to a river flowing out of the dense Wealden forest.

One of the Burghal Hidage manuscripts preserved provides a formula for calculating how many hides are required to defend a given length of wall, which works out to four men per "pole", a measure of about five metres. *Eorpeburnan*'s hidage was 324, which gives us some 400 metres of wall. This is about right, if we assume that the wall needing defence is the western side, towards the rest of the peninsula, and that the three other sides did not require defence because they were impassable tidal marshes. Having said that, it seems somewhat risky to assume this, if we are talking about defending the site against water-borne attackers. Maybe this was why the fort was so easily taken by the Danes in 892? On the other hand, the relationship between hidage and length of defences is not exact at other sites either. Perhaps the relatively low hidage just reflects that the surrounding area was only sparsely populated. It is also possible that Alfred's *burh*-builders decided to adopt a pre-existing Iron Age fortification instead of following exactly the required hidage.

The later works

Strictly speaking, the name Castle Toll should only apply to the later, still prominent works. These are sometimes described as a "motte and bailey" castle, but this seems unlikely. The motte and bailey design was brought to England by the Normans, and consists of a "motte", being a mound of earth, on which was usually built a keep of stone, next to a "bailey" which was a courtyard enclosed by a ditch and a palisade. These were built in the 11th and early 12th centuries by the Normans to control the surrounding area. They were quickly constructed, but were soon replaced by more formidable structures. By the mid-12th century, they had gone out of fashion in England.

Hasted in 1798 writes of this fort that it is

> a piece of ground raised much higher than the former; this was encompassed with a double ditch, the traces of which are still visible in some places, and within the innermost of them is somewhat more than an acre of land. The shape is a square, with the corners a little rounded; and at each corner, within the area, is a circular mount of earth.

The square shape remains, but the only circular mount of earth remaining is the north-eastern one, the others presumably having been lost to the plough, or deliberately removed to facilitate working the land. This if we are to believe Hasted's description, but other early historians, such as Harris in *History of Kent*[110], also refer to more than one mound of earth.

When the Ministry of Works excavated the site in the 1960's, they concluded that these works had been occupied for two short periods in the early and mid-13th century, perhaps as a watch-post to look out for raiders coming up the river. The difficulty with this theory is to think of any raiders that might have been coming to the Weald at that time. The Vikings had long since given up and French raiding did not start in earnest for another 100 years.

That is not to say there wasn't any warfare involving England. At the beginning of the century, King John was busily losing Normandy and the rest of the Angevin lands to King Philip II of France, but those battles took place on the other side of the Channel. After John failed to live up to his undertakings in the Magna Carta, the barons started a civil war against John, and invited Philip's son Louis to become king of England. He duly landed in Kent and met very little resistance, except at Dover Castle (which he never took). Soon, he controlled most of southern England. However, when King John died in 1216, the barons shifted their allegiance to his young son, Henry, and threw Louis out. These battles did not involve the kind of raiding against which one might build a small river fortification.

A reasonable peace was concluded with the Treaty of Lambeth, and the French then were largely at peace with England until the 14th century.

King Henry eventually developed trouble with the barons, too. In 1262, Simon de Montfort led the barons in war against Henry and soon captured most of the south-east. The people of Winchelsea were particularly strong supporters of the Montfort side. In the Battle of Lewes, 1264, Henry was captured and held prisoner, together with his son Edward, who would later be King Edward I (see above). Later, Edward escaped, rallied the troops and eventually, de Montfort was killed at the Battle of Evesham in 1265, after which Henry resumed power and took harsh revenge on the rebels.

However, while Henry and Edward were held by the rebel side, Queen Eleanor (of Provence, Henry's wife) was in France, raising a fleet and army to come to her husband's support. She was successful enough in the summer of 1264, that de Montfort and his allies felt compelled to raise a large peasant army in Kent to guard against any invasion from France[iii]. In the end, Queen Eleanor's forces never materialised, but could this have been the time when a fortification was hastily improvised at Castle Toll by the local defenders?

As with so many other aspects of Newenden's history, we will probably never know, and the real history will remain a rich subject of speculation for historians, amateur and professional alike.

Appendix

Rectors of Newenden[112]

Also some other incumbents.

	From, or first mention	Until, or last mention
Richard de Wenchepe	1272	
Robert de Askeby	1294	
William de Kensington	1305	
William de Bereham		Resigned 1313
William de St Albans	1313	1317
Ade de Radbrok	1317	1318
John de Naverby	1318	
John Ffoucher	1327	
Henry de Southchurch	1340	
Thomas de Uffington	1362	
Richard Laurence	1396	
Jacob de Colesford		1399

	From, or first mention	Until, or last mention
John Iflen(?)	1399	
John Dunton	1403	
John Creyt	1406	
John Hunt	1407	
William S.?		1495
Thomas Mandisley	1495	
Sir John Parker	1523	
Sir Walter Barknell	1525	
Sir John Welles	1540	1546
Robert Walmersley	1546	1562
Peter Hall	1562	Buried Newenden 13 May 1566
Lawrence Smyth	1568	1572
John Tunbridge	1572	Buried Newenden 4 Nov 1609
John Hopton	Vicar 1584	
Richard White	1609	1642
William Hieron	1661	
Thomas Brown	1662	Resigned 1664
Walter Collins	Inducted 26 Jan 1665	
James Kay	Inducted July 1668	
John Maccorne	Curate 1674	
David Maccorne	1676	Buried Newenden 19 Jan 1687

	From, or first mention	Until, or last mention
James Stretton	1687	Resigned 1694 (also Vicar of Rolvenden)
Thomas Fishenden	1694	1737 (Vicar of Rolvenden, buried there)
Robert Gascoyne	1737	1738
William Hudleston	1738	Buried Newenden 13 June 1743 (gravestone in north-west corner of church floor)
Richard Morton	1743	Buried "within the altar rails" 1772
Thomas Morphett	1772	1812 (also Vicar of Rolvenden)
John Pechey Francis	1812	1855[113]
James Boys	Curate 1816	
Thomas Brown	Curate 1817	
James Monypenny	Curate 1824	
John Wilson	Curate 1828	
Robert Twigg	Curate 1831	
John Pugh or Pughe	1855	1878
William Greenhill	1879	1894
Edmund Jermyn	1894	1897
John Henry Burrows	1897	1920
Thomas Gilbert Beal	1920	1945 (with Sandhurst)
Harry Jackman	1945	1948

Appendix

	From, or first mention	Until, or last mention
Arthur Culmer	1948	1960
Anthony Harbottle	1960	1968
John Green	1968	1990
Richard Dengate	1990	2001
Anthea Williams	2001	2004 (with Rolvenden)
Jacques Desrosiers	2004	

Maps

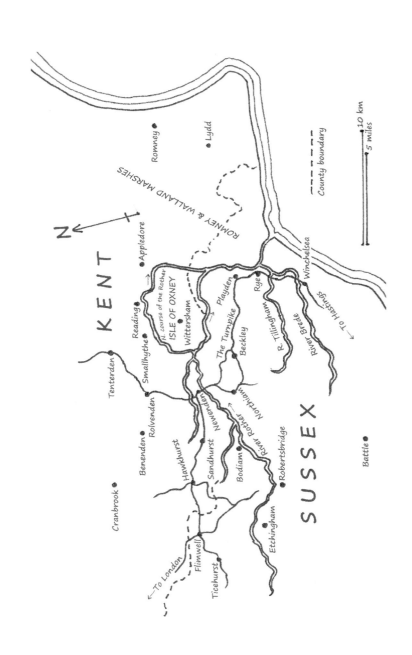

KENT

SUSSEX

ROMNEY & WALLAND MARSHES

ISLE OF OXNEY

N. course of the Rother

Romney

Lydd

Appledore

Reading

Smallhythe

Wittersham

The Turnpike

Playden

Rye

Winchelsea

To Hastings

Beckley

R. Tillingham

River Brede

Tenterden

Benenden

Rolvenden

Newenden

Northiam

River Rother

Hawkhurst

Sandhurst

Bodiam

Robertsbridge

Cranbrook

Etchingham

Battle

Flimwell

To London

Ticehurst

N

County boundary

5 miles

10 km

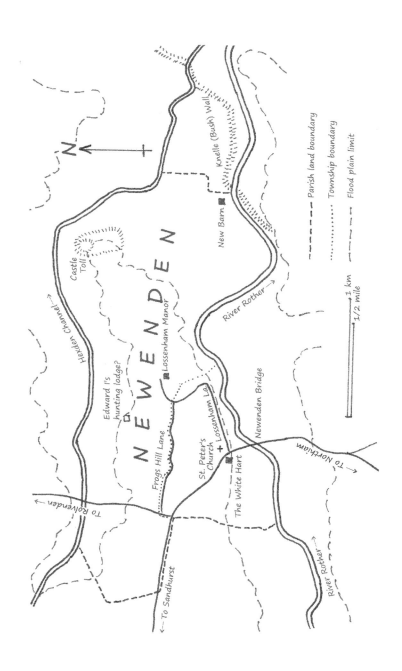

N

NEWENDEN

Castle Toll

Hexden Channel →

Edward I's hunting lodge?

■ Lossenham Manor

Frogs Hill Lane

Knelle (Bush) Wall

New Barn ■

River Rother →

Lossenham La.

St. Peter's Church

Newenden Bridge

The White Hart

To Rolvenden ←

To Sandhurst ←

To Northiam →

River Rother →

- - - - Parish land boundary
·········· Township boundary
- · - · - Flood plain limit

1 km
1/2 mile

St. Peter's church (outline)

Chancel (1300)

Tower (1300)

Lady chapel

Chancel (1450–51)

Base of pillar

North aisle rebuilt (15th C?)

South aisle rebuilt (15th C?)

Blanking wall (1701)

North aisle

Nave

South aisle

Porch

Turret (1858)

Tower (1701)

Present walls

Known walls post–1700

Conjectured walls pre–1700

10m (Approx. scale)

30ft

Notes

Abbreviations in the notes

BRS	British Record Society
CCA	Canterbury Cathedral Archives
ESRO	East Sussex Record Office
KAS	Kent Archaeological Society
KHLC	Kent History and Library Centre (formerly Centre for Kentish Studies)
LPL	Lambeth Palace Library
Nat. Arch.	National Archives (Kew)

Where the notes refer to an author only, the reference is to be taken to the work of that author listed in the Bibliography.

Unpublished sources are shown with their respective archive references.

Notes

Origins

1 Peter Sawyer, *Anglo-Saxon Charters: an Annotated List and Bibliography*, Royal Historical Society 1968. Charter number 1614, in Canterbury, Christ Church. The Anglo-Saxon charters have been made extremely easily accessible on the Web, see <http://www.esawyer.org.uk>

2 *[A]nno dominice incarnationis .dccxci. Ego Offa rex concedo ecclesie Christi Cantuarie terram iuris mei .xv. aratrorum in prouincia Cantie in hiis postnominatis locis, id est Iecham, Perhamstede, Rochinga, et in saltu qui dicitur Andred pascua porcorum in hiis locis, Dunwalingden, Sandhyrste, Swithelmingden, et in siluis que dicuntur Bocholt et Blean Heanhric et aliud inter torrentem nomine neorthburnan et hagenatreou et pastum unius gregis iuxta Theningden, . et .l. porcorum binnan snæde. Hanc predictam donacionem concedo, ecclesie Christi cum omnibus ad eam rite pertinentibus liberam ab omni regali tributo. Si quis uero hoc donum meum infringere temptauerit, perpetuo anathemate feriatur.*

3 By the author – apologies for any infelicities.

4 Some later authorities (even Hasted), noting the impressive lack of the name Newenden, have tried claiming that Andred – the ancient name for the Wealden forest – is an alias for Newenden. But the wording of the charter clearly refers to a forest called Andred, in which Dunwalingden and the others are located, not to a village.

5 Nonetheless, it was correctly read as Dunwalingden already by Somner in 1693 – p.109.

6 William Lambarde, 1536–1601, wrote (in 1570) *Perambulation of Kent*, the first English county history.

7 Sawyer number 123; this is a longer text, but the properties are more or less the same, including *"Dunualing daenn Sandhyrst Suiðhelming daenn"*

8 Barbara Yorke, *Kings and Kingdoms of Early Anglo-Saxon*

England, Routledge 1990, p.43

9   Sawyer number 39.

10   The old name for the Rother.

11   Eilert Ekwall, *The Concise Oxford Dictionary of English Place-names*, 4th edition, OUP 1960, p.304

12   J. K. Wallenberg, *The Place-Names of Kent*, Uppsala 1934

13   Stenton, p.59

14   British Library, Cotton manuscripts, Aug. II 36, transcribed in Flight p.214

15   British Library, Cotton manuscripts, Claudius C, vi fo. 165 v., transcribed in Flight p.217

16   *The Archaeological Journal*, vol. 15 1858, p.165

17   The great inventory of manors in England was drawn up by order of William I and finalised in 1086.

Market

18   Lawson & Killingray, p.50

19   For a useful summary with examples of mediaeval market practices, see Helen Douglas-Irvine, *Extracts relating to mediaeval markets and fairs in England*, MacDonald & Evans 1912

20   Domesday Book in translation: "The Archbishop holds Newenden for himself. It answers for one sulung. [sulh being the Old English word for a plough, a sulung was the land that could be ploughed by a team of 8 oxen, about 200-240 acres] There are 25 villagers with 4 smallholders who have 5 ploughs. A market worth 40s less 5d. Woodland, 40 pigs. In total valued at £100 in the days of Rex Edward [Confessor]. When acquired £12, now £10 but the reeve pays £18 10s."

21   Faversham was also a bigger place itself, having 30 villagers, 40 smallholders, 5 slaves, a mill, 100 pigs, 2 salt-houses and was worth £80.

Notes

22 Record Commissioners, *Placita de Quo Warranto*, 1818, p.324 – this is a transcription of Eyre Rolls from the reigns of Edward I through to Edward III.

23 CCA – reference missing

24 Darby, pp.32-33

25 There are many ways of spelling this surname, but this is what the modern spelling would be; "Dalyngrygge" seems to have been quite popular at the time.

26 Calendar of Charter Rolls, Richard II

27 Patent Rolls of Richard II. It is sometimes said that Sir Edward only was granted the right to fortify his manor house, and that he took it upon himself to build the castle without permission. But the wording of the licence seems quite clear – to fortify the mansion and build a castle.

River, road and bridge

28 Eric Pawson, *Transport and Economy: The Turnpike Roads of Eighteenth Century Britain*, Academic Press, 1977

29 ESRO – PAR 431/24/1

30 Friday St was so named because it was where the fish market was. The Saracen's Head Inn was apparently quite a large establishment, also the starting place for coaches to Taunton and Yeovil.

31 Consols are old Government bonds (gilts), first issued in 1751. Unusually, they are perpetual, i.e. they do not carry a fixed redemption date, and so they were considered suitable investments for perpetual trusts, such as Wilford's Charity.

32 Registration numbers 223943 for the Kent charity and 237842 for the Sussex one.

33 For this and the continued historical development of the river, the descriptions in Goodison in particular, but also Cardwell and Collard have been especially helpful. The time-line in Barry Yates and Patrick Triplet: *Two bays, one environment – a shared*

biodiversity with a common focus, a report of the Interreg II project, Dec 2000 (can be found at <http://www.wildrye.info/files/Changes in Rye Bay.pdf>) is also very handy.

34 Patent Rolls of Henry III, 3 May 1256

35 Patent Rolls of Edward III.

36 Darby, p.32

37 There also used to be a sluice in the Rother just above its confluence with Newmill Channel, called Newenden sluice: L.A. Edwards, *Inland Waterways of Great Britain*, 6th ed, Imray Laurie Norie & Wilson, 1985. This was for the purpose of drainage control, rather than for navigational reasons. I believe it was built some time after commercial navigation ceased and became superfluous when the new flood defences were built in the 1970s. The stoneworks can still be seen from a boat.

38 Vine, p.41 ff.

39 In the letter mentioned above note 33, also Eddison, p.106

40 Patent Rolls of Edward III, 16 June 1365.

41 Camden p.351

42 ESRO – QR/E 38 fo. 1

43 KHLC – U386/O2/3

44 All of these and following orders in KHLC – Q/AB 42

45 Curiously, the bridge is, at the time of writing, listed twice: once in Kent, as a Grade II building, and once in East Sussex, listed as Grade II*. This state of affairs has prevailed for over 50 years, but will now be reviewed by English Heritage.

46 An original print of the Act is preserved at ESRO – ACC 2449/1/15

47 ESRO – QDT/EW1

48 ESRO – Q/Rut/40

Edward I and his friends

49 Pratt, p.35

50 Morris, p.75

51 Pratt, p.42

52 Pratt, p.61

53 Morris, p.368 and Pratt pp.66-67

54 You will sometimes see the year quoted as 1300, but that would be according to the old reckoning, where the New Year started on 25 March. This causes an awful lot of confusion in history writing – I have tried to convert all years to new reckoning but can't promise I have got them all right.

55 Yes, really – for example in Kilburne, p.198

56 For this and the subsequent description of the Auchers, see *The Essex Review: An Illustrated Quarterly Record of Everything of Permanent Interest in the County*, Volume 6, E. Durant and Company, 1897, p. 91 ff.

57 Patent Rolls of Edward I, 25 November 1275

58 William Page (Ed.), *Victoria County History, Kent*, Vol. 2, The St. Catherine Press, 1926, pp.203-4

59 Pratt, p.43

60 Morris, p.201

61 The following story of the Waleys family is based on the summary of the Glynde Place archives at ESRO, *The Glynde Place archives: a catalogue*, by Richard F. Dell, 1964.

62 KAS, *Kent Hundred Rolls Project*, Bridgett Jones 2007

63 Nat. Arch. SC 1/21/76

64 Joan married Adam de Petstede and as dower was granted a third of the deer in Glynde park, by assignment of a certain William de Marreys (I presume he must have been Joan's guardian in some way). This William, together with others, then came and hunted in the park, and took away deer. The Petstede

couple issued a writ of trespass against William, who claimed this was invalid as the deer were held in common and anyway it was his park. But Chief Justice Brabazon held that the writ was valid as she had full rights to a third of the deer. See Baker and Milsom: *Sources of English Legal History: Private Law to 1750*, 2nd edition, OUP 2010 p. 339.

Population

65 Nat. Arch. E179

66 Nat. Arch. E179/123/12

67 H.A. Hanley and C.W. Chalklin (Ed.): *Kent Lay Subsidy of 1334/5*, KAS 1961 and 2008

68 Ibid. p.5

69 Mark Gardiner in Eddison, Gardner and Long, ch. 8

70 Mary J. Dobson in Eddison, Gardner and Long, ch. 10

71 Duncan W. Harrington (Ed.), *Kent hearth tax assessment, Lady Day 1664*, BRS Hearth Tax Series II, 2000

72 KHLC – Q/RPI/265

73 KHLC – P264/27

74 ESRO – RYE/47/9/(18)

75 A sennight is a week – it is a contraction of "seven nights", analogous with fortnight. But much less used nowadays.

76 ESRO – FRE/28

77 ESRO – LRD 1/2/1

Manors, Township and Liberty

78 Stenton, p.480 ff.

79 The Anglo-Saxons called the city *Cantwaraburh* – the *burh* (or borough) of the Men of Kent. *War* or *wer* is an old Germanic word for man, which you can still find in werewolf – literally a

man-wolf. Since w is a double-u, you will now understand why
the Archbishops sign themselves *Cantuar*.

80   Stenton, pp.148-149

81   As with most Kentish manors, they did not hold the manor
directly from the king, but through a chain of overlords. It
appears their immediate lord was the Earl of Hereford, who at
this time was Humphrey de Bohun, one of Edward I's
godparents. He held the manor from the Countess of Eu, who
held it from the Earl of Arundel – at this time Hugh d'Aubigny,
whose ancestors had been granted it by William I himself – at
least if I understand Flight, p.249 correctly.

82   Hasted. His description of the early history of the Auchers may
have to be taken *cum grano salis*.

83   Might this be Earl Leofric of Mercia, I wonder, who was a
contemporary and sometime rival of Godwin?

84   Flight, p.50

85   ESRO – GLY/954 refers to the Waleys family holding a knight's
fee (= a manor) from the Archbishop at Lossenham at various
times, but this can't be right – the Auchers were at Lossenham
and the Archbishop was not the overlord there. Which goes to
show how closely related the two manors are.

86   Hasted.

87   Sussex has sub-divisions called "rapes" but they are thought to
be later than the Kentish lathes.

88   Beresford and Finberg, p. 29

89   KHLC – P/264/5/1

90   This and following minute in KHLC – P264/8/A/1

Church

91   See also Flight, ch. 8

92   There is a St Martin's in Canterbury, which is the oldest English
parish church in continuous use, dating back to the 6th century,

but that is presumably not the one referred to. Aldington St Martin is the most likely candidate.

93 CCA – Ch Ant D 43

94 Pub. by G. Eyre and A. Strahan, *Taxatio ecclesiastica Angliae et Walliae, auctoritate P. Nicholai IV, circa A.D.1291* in 1802.

95 KAS – *Medieval & Tudor Kent P.C.C. Wills, Transcriptions* by L. L. Duncan, Book 60: John Barker, p.27 and John Twisden, p.28.

96 CCA – VC 111/46/33

97 KHLC – P264/5/1

98 William Henry Ireland: *England's topographer, or A new and complete history of the county of Kent...*, G. Virtue 1828, Vol. 3 p. 122

99 If you want to be technical: argent, on a bend gules surmounted by a bend argent, three trefoils sable.

100 KHLC – P264/5/2

101 Roper, p.6

102 KHLC – P264/6/B/2

103 KHLC – P264/5/2

104 CCA – D/T/N/5

105 KHLC – P264/5

Castle Toll

106 Castle Toll is listed by English Heritage as a Scheduled Monument at Risk, due to ploughing, with the trend being listed as Declining. Go and see it now, before it disappears altogether...

107 The Anglo-Saxon Chronicle exists in nine slightly different manuscripts from mediaeval times, and has been translated and published on several occasions. A recent scholarly translation is G.H. Garmonsway (Ed.): *The Anglo-Saxon Chronicles*, Phoenix Press, 1990. It is the story of the Anglo-Saxon people in England

from the beginnings to the mid-12th century. It is most conveniently accessed on the web – see <http://omacl.org/Anglo/>

108 In this context; it could also mean a (walled) town.

109 For example Gillian Draper, in *Rye: A History of a Sussex Cinque Port to 1660*, p.2

110 John Harris, *History of Kent*, London 1719.

111 Morris, p.64

Appendix

112 Older entries from LPL – Act books of the Archbishops, later ones from Jermyn and/or Roper.

113 This poor man "shot himself in his study while temporarily insane" – retrieved from the *Clergy of the Church of England* database at <http://www.theclergydatabase.org.uk>. He was also Rector of St. Peter's and Vicar of Westgate, both in Canterbury (and his study was there).

Bibliography

Beresford, Maurice and Finberg, H.P.R.: *English Medieval Boroughs: a handlist*, David & Charles, 1973

Camden, William: *Britannia*, Andrew Crooke, 1637

Cardwell, Tony: *Limen – A biography of the East Sussex Rother*, The Wealden Advertiser, 2001

Collard, John: *A Maritime History of Rye*, Facer Publishing, 1985

Darby, Ben: *Journey through the Weald*, St Edmundsbury Press, 1986

Eddison, Jill: *Romney Marsh – Survival on a Frontier*, Tempus Publishing, 2000

Eddison, Jill, Gardiner, Mark and Long, Anthony J. (Ed.): *Romney Marsh: Environmental Change and Human Occupation in a Coastal Lowland*, Oxford University Committee for Archaeology, 1998

Flight, Colin: *The survey of Kent: documents relating to the survey of the county conducted in 1086*, British Archaeological Reports, 2010

Goodsall, Robert H.: *The Eastern Rother*, Constable and Company, 1961

Hasted, Edward: *The History and Topographical Survey of the County of Kent*, Vol. 7, 1798

Holloway, William: *The History of Romney Marsh and its*

Bibliography

Adjacencies, from its Earliest Formation to 1837, John Russell Smith, 1849

Jermyn, Edmund (Ed.): *The Register of Newenden, Co. Kent*, The Parish Register Society, 1897

Kilburne, Richard: *A topographie or survey of the county of Kent*, Henry Atkinson, 1659

Lawson, Terence & Killingray, David (Ed.): *An historical atlas of Kent*, Phillimore & Co., 2004

Morgan, Philip (Ed.): *Domesday Book, 1: Kent*, Phillimore & Co., 1983

Morris, Marc: *A Great and Terrible King*, Windmill Books, 2009

Pratt, Malcolm: *Winchelsea – the tale of a medieval town*, M. Pratt, 2005

Roper, Anne: *The Church of Saint Peter, Newenden*, 1993

Somner, William: *A Treatise of the Roman Ports and Forts in Kent*, J. Brome, 1693

Spelling, R.S.: *Newenden – A Pictorial History of a Village on the Kent and East Sussex Border*, R.S. Spelling, 1988

Stenton, Frank: *Anglo-Saxon England*, Oxford University Press, 3rd Ed. 1971

Vine, P.A.L.: *Kent & East Sussex Waterways*, Middleton Press, 1989

Witney, K.P.: *The Jutish Forest: A Study of the Weald of Kent from 450 A.D. to 1380 A.D.*, Athlone Press, 1976

Index

Index

Index

Index

Index

Index

FRIENDS OF SAINT PETER'S CHURCH, NEWENDEN

Like many village churches, Saint Peter's Church in Newenden on the Kent/East Sussex border is an important landmark and a vital part of the community. It is not only a place of worship but also a beautiful building of immense historical importance.

However, in a small village like Newenden, the regular maintenance of such an old building consumes all available funds, and additional money is urgently required to preserve the fabric of the church.

The Friends charity was set up in February 2003 so that everybody can contribute to the preservation of Saint Peter's as a historical and architectural monument, without any religious implications. Repair and restoration projects are funded after consultation with the Parochial Church Council.

Contributions to the Friends are welcomed from all sources: current and former residents and their families, regular church goers, people who have used the church for christenings, weddings and funerals, visitors to Newenden and anyone with a wish to preserve a part of our heritage.

PATRON: HH Judge Diana Faber
Registered Charity No. 1098260